Visiting

NORTH CAROLINA

STATE PARKS

Visiting NORTH CAROLINA STATE PARKS

A Guide to the State Parks in North Carolina

J.L. and Lin Stepp

Mountain Hill Press

A Division of S & S Communications

Visiting North Carolina State Parks
Copyright © 2023
James L. Stepp

Cover Design by Katherine E. Stepp
Cover Photos by J.L. and Lin Stepp
Book Design and Layout by Mountain Hill Press
Editorial Assistance by Elizabeth S. James
Interior Photos by J.L and Lin Stepp

Published by Mountain Hill Press
A division of S & S Communications

Author note. This is a non-fiction guidebook created by the authors based on their visitations and research of North Carolina State Parks. Effort has been made to ensure accuracy of specific environs and place names, but places and names may change over time as do descriptive trail details.

Library of Congress Cataloging-in-Publication Data

Stepp, J.L. and Lin
   Visiting North Carolina State Parks: A Guide to the State Parks in North Carolina

   ISBN 979-8-9877251-0-8
   eISBN 979-8-9877251-1-5

Non-Fiction. 1. State Parks—North Carolina—Guidebooks. 2. Parks—Southeast—Guide books. 3. Travel—North Carolina—Guidebooks.
      I. Stepp, J.L. and Lin II. Title
      Library of Congress Control Number: 2023910684

ACKNOWLEDGMENTS

Thanks and gratitude go to the North Carolina Department of Parks and Recreation located in Raleigh, North Carolina. We are deeply grateful for:
- Their mission to inspire all visitors through conservation, recreation and education; to conserve and protect the natural beauty, ecological features, recreational and cultural resources within the parks system; to provide and promote enjoyable, healthy, and safe outdoor recreational opportunities; and to provide educational opportunities to promote good stewardship of North Carolina's natural and cultural heritage;
- Their website detailing each of the forty-two state parks, which helped us with the accuracy of our book (Website link: www.ncparks.gov);
- Their care in maintaining all the parks throughout the state of North Carolina, making each a pleasure to visit.

Additional thanks go to the North Carolina branch of the National Park Service, located in Washington DC, for their:
- Part in preserving, protecting, and managing scenic areas not only in the state of North Carolina but around the US;
- Efforts to maintain and preserve unique historic and natural sites in the state, that we enjoyed visiting and included in this guidebook

Appreciation and thanks also go to:
- The park rangers and visitor center staff in each park we visited, who answered questions and helped us with information at our park visits.

Discovering
TENNESSEE
STATE PARKS
A Guide to the State Parks in Tennessee
J.L. and Lin Stepp

THE
Afternoon
HIKER
A GUIDE TO CASUAL HIKES IN THE
GREAT SMOKY MOUNTAINS
J.L. AND LIN STEPP

Exploring
SOUTH CAROLINA
STATE PARKS
A Guide to the State Parks in South Carolina
J.L. and Lin Stepp

Introduction

At the time of publication of this book, we now have four published regional guidebooks, a hiking guide and three state park guides. Our journey of writing guidebooks began while hiking in the Great Smoky Mountains Park near our home. We'd always visited in the park with our kids, but now, with an empty nest and more leisure time, we discovered hiking in a new way. The trail guides we purchased seemed geared to more veteran hikers than us, often provided unclear directions to the trailheads and information we really didn't need. So we decided to write our own guidebook suitable for non-Sierra types like ourselves, looking for easily accessible, enjoyable hikes that could be completed in an afternoon. *The Afternoon Hiker*, published in 2014, was the result, describing 110 trails in the Smoky Mountains with color photos throughout.

In 2014, a U.S. Government shut down of all the national parks, including the Smokies, led us to investigate area state parks as an alternative hiking option for our weekend getaways. After not locating any guidebooks with the park-by-park descriptions we hoped for, we decided to write our own. Over the next two years we visited all 56 of the state parks in Tennessee, creating a guidebook similar in format to our hiking guide. The book, *Discovering Tennessee State Parks* published in 2018 and provides directions to and descriptions of every park in Tennessee with over 700 color photos in illustration.

A few years later in 2019, while vacationing in South Carolina, and doing bookstore signings around the area for Lin's latest novel set at Edisto, many of our fans and readers—and several bookstore managers, where we had scheduled events, encouraged us to consider writing a similar parks guidebook for South Carolina. After a little thought we decided to do so and started a new adventure visiting and exploring all the South Carolina state parks, National Parks and historic sites, resulting in our 2021 guidebook *Exploring South Carolina State Parks*.

Before this book was completed and published, bookstores and fans began to encourage us to also do a state parks guidebook for North Carolina. So, over the next two years, around our other work, we traveled to all of the state parks and national parks in North Carolina, starting on the coast in the Tidewater region and working out way west to the Mountains region of the state. With each park visited, we included directions to get to the site, a description of the park, its sections and amenities, trails to hike, things to do and see, and we noted the month we visited—since different seasons offer different pleasures in the parks. In addition, we included hundreds of color photos throughout the book to give readers a flavor of what they might see at their visits. The resulting book *Visiting North Carolina State Parks*, is the perfect companion for those wanting to visit and explore any or all of North Carolina's parks. We hope readers will use and cherish this guidebook as they tour and enjoy the interesting and scenic variety of parks scattered across the state.

If you plan to visit many—or all—of North Carolina's state parks, pick up a *North Carolina State Parks Passport* booklet. The Passport booklet allows visitors to keep track of their state park adventures across the state. Collect a stamp for each park and see if you can get them all! Pick up a free copy of the Passport book at a state park office or visitor center. Please contact the park beforehand to make sure they have the books available.

TABLE OF CONTENTS

Goose Creek State Park	14	Occoneechee Mountain State Park	104
Fort Raleigh National Historic Site	18	Jordan Lake State Park	106
Jockey's Ridge State Park	22	Guilford Courthouse Military Park	110
Pettigrew State Park	26	Haw River State Park	112
Wright Brothers National Memorial	30	Mayo River State Park	114
Cape Hatteras National Seashore	32	Morrow Mountain State Park	116
Cape Lookout National Seashore	36	Hanging Rock State Park	120
Carolina Beach State Park	40	Lake Norman State Park	124
Fort Fisher State Historic Park	44	Crowders Mountain State Park	128
Fort Macon State Park	48	Pilot Mountain State Park	132
Hammocks Beach State Park	52	New River State Park	136
Moores Creek National Battlefield	54	Mount Jefferson State Park	138
Dismal Swamp State Park	60	Stone Mountain State Park	140
Merchants Millpond State Park	62	Elk Knob State Park	144
Lumber River State Park	64	South Mountains State Park	146
Lake Waccamaw State Park	66	Lake James State Park	148
Singletary Lake State Park	70	Overmountain Victory Historic Park	152
Jones Lake State Park	72	Blue Ridge Parkway	154
Cliffs of the Neuse State Park	76	Mount Mitchell State Park	158
Medoc Mountain State Park	80	Grandfather Mountain State Park	160
Carvers Creek State Park	82	Carl Sandburg Historic Site	164
Raven Rock State Park	84	Chimney Rock State Park	166
Weymouth Woods State Park	86	Appalachian Trail	170
Kerr Lake State Park	90	Rendezvous Mountain State Park	172
William B. Umstead State Park	94	Trail of Tears Historic Trail	174
Falls Lake State Park	98	Gorges State Park	176
Eno River State Park	102	Great Smoky Mountains Nat'l Park	180

HISTORY OF STATE PARKS

The history of the state and national parks are intertwined. State parks, like national ones, were established to preserve locations of natural beauty and recreational potential and to safeguard places of historic significance. The first national park, Yellowstone National Park, was established by an Act of Congress in 1872 and signed by President Ulysses Grant, beginning the national parks movement. More parks followed, especially out west, before Southern ones began to develop. President Theodore Roosevelt was a great champion in advancing the national park movement, and many bird and game preserves, national forests, parks, and monuments were established during his presidency.

The first state park was Niagara Falls State Park, established in 1885, with a few others following in the late 1800s and early 1900s. In 1921, at the request of Stephen Mather, National Park Service Director, a group of preservationists and conservationists met in Iowa to discuss the concept of developing additional parks at the state level. This 1921 National Conference of State Parks, hosted by the National Park Service, spurred interest in developing more sites around America and initiated the state park movement. At the time of the conference twenty-nine states, including South Carolina, had no parks, but by 1925, all forty-eight states had begun to formulate development plans. Although the beginning of the Depression slowed growth, many recreational areas were developed later in the 1930s through Depression-era programs like the Civilian Conservation Corps (CCC) and the Works Progress Administration (WPA). States around the U.S. recognized that lands needed to be preserved at the local level that would not become designated as national sites. By 1972, every state in the U.S. had a state parks system.

North Carolina's state parks, like others in America, were created to preserve and protect unique recreational, historic, cultural, and scenic natural areas. In North Carolina in 1891, the U.S. Geological Survey did a study to examine timber and mineral resources in the state. This report brought to the state's attention how much damage was occurring across the state with timbering and mining. The state began to look at ways to conserve and preserve natural resources. Citizens near the Mount Mitchell area began to push for the state to save the mountain and land being overly logged, and those efforts resulted in the General Assembly creating the state's first official state park—Mount Mitchell in 1915. Interest in expanding the state park system grew after this and in 1924 the state opened Fort Macon, the state's second park, with more soon following.

A Department of Conservation and Development was created to handle the new parks and several other state legislative actions soon brought many of the state's lakes into the state park system. A boon to park development happened when President Yent Roosevelt created the Civilian Conservations Corps (CCC) and other public works programs in the 1930s, sending workers into the states to help to build park roads and buildings. Many other parks were created in this era, too, like Morrow Mountain, Hanging Rock State Park, Jones Lake, the William Umstead State Park, Pettigrew State Park, and more. World War II (1941-1945) stalled park development but after the war the State Recreation Commission was created and new appropriations allowed more parks to develop, like Cliffs of the Neuse. Growth of new parks grew slowly but steadily over the years to come and soon natural and recreation areas also began to be added to the park system.

In time, expansion slowed, but in the 1980s the General Assembly appropriated more monies for expansion of the parks system. During this time the purpose of the State Parks system was clarified and new legislative actions and local support helped move development and growth of the parks system forward again, which continued into the 1990s. Workers were increased for the parks and new management plans created. Budget shortfalls hurt park expansion in the 2000s but gradually studies for needed improvements were made. and at the park's 90th anniversary more advancements occurred, including the addition of still more parks.

Today the state has 42 state parks, and is constantly working to upgrade and develop many of its parks' visitor centers, campgrounds, and properties, as well as continuing to bring new parks on board. In particular, more parks are being added in the western North Carolina area, and plans are underway to open a new park, the Pisgah View State Park, in the next few years. The Division of Parks and Recreation lists six types of parks included in the overall North Carolina State Parks System—State Parks, State Lakes, State Recreation Areas, State Trails, State Natural Areas, and State Rivers—but these are not all managed under the same department.

The NC Division of Parks and Recreation manages over 250,000 acres now and welcomes over 22 million visitors a year. There is no charge to visit most of North Carolina's state parks and most parks are open year-round. Their stated mission is "to inspire all its citizens and visitors through conservation, recreation, and education." The main park office is in Raleigh, North Carolina, with phone numbers, and address contacts on the *ncparks.gov* website.

"In every walk with nature one receives far more than he seeks." – John Muir

"Earth and sky, woods and fields, lakes and river, the mountains and the sea,
are excellent school masters, and teach some of us more than we can
ever learn from books." – John Lubbock

Carolina Beach

TIDEWATER REGION STATE PARK INDEX

Goose Creek State Park **14**
Fort Raleigh National Historic Site **18**
Jockey's Ridge State Park **22**
Pettigrew State Park **26**
Wright Brothers National Memorial **30**
Cape Hatteras National Seashore **32**
Cape Lookout National Seashore **36**
Carolina Beach State Park **40**
Fort Fisher State Historic Site **44**
Fort Macon State Park **48**
Hammocks Beach State Park **52**
Moores Creek National Battlefield **54**

Tidewater Region
North Carolina
PARKS

Jockey's Ridge

Goose Creek

Fort Macon

Hammocks Beach

Goose Creek State Park

Park Address: 2190 Camp Leach Rd, Washington, NC 27889

Park Size: 1,672 acres   Month Visited: June

Directions: From I-95, take Hwy 264 East. Pass through Washington and follow for 10 miles to Camp Leach Road. Turn right and travel about 2.5 miles to the park entrance.

Park Description:

Goose Creek is a scenic park with a lot of diversity on the Pamlico River, which winds from the park into the Pamlico Sound and Atlantic Ocean. The park, which opened in 1974, has over nine miles of shoreline on the river and along Goose Creek, and the views across the wide Pamlico River are gorgeous. The park has camping, hiking, swimming, picnicking, and boating opportunities, all in a peaceful rural setting.

After entering the park, stop first at the Environmental Education and Visitor Center. Here you can get park maps, information, and watch a five-minute film to introduce you to Goose Creek Park. You will also find interactive wetland exhibits, animal displays, aquariums, and other scenic learning centers. Outside, you can see a butterfly garden and a bird observation station.

The park has nine trails that wander through different areas. You'll find the first, the Palmetto Boardwalk Trail, right behind the visitor center. It's a short, easy, half-mile walk that winds into the woods and wetlands across a long boardwalk. The trail passes a screened-in outdoor classroom where programs are often given. A second trail, beginning near the visitor center, is the easy Long Leaf Trail that loops for 1.3

miles through the woods and back. A picnic area and shelter can also be found near the visitor center and trails.

Continuing down the main road leads to the park's new campground area with 22 sites for RV camping with full hookups, picnic tables, fire rings with grills, and a bathhouse. There are six camper cabins at the RV campground that can be rented. The cabins don't have bathrooms but share the nearby bathhouse with the RV campers.

Turning to drive down Campground Road leads to 14 more spacious campsites for tent camping. Along Campground Road you'll also find the Ivey Gut Trail that wanders through the pine woods and along the shore of Goose Creek. At the end of the Campground Road at the loop turnaround, the Goose Creek Trail and the Flatty Creek Trail begin, both offering nice views across the creek and river. There are overlooks, rest benches, and picnic tables along the point as well as a long fishing pier to enjoy. We found this to be a very scenic site.

Across the lake from the end of the Campground Road, you can see Dinah's Landing on the other side of Goose Creek, where boats and other

water craft can be launched. This section of the park is reached from a second entrance on the other side of Goose Creek off Camp Leach Road. There are picnic tables, grills, and shelters there to enjoy. Dinah's Landing is a good spot for canoe or kayak paddlers to launch their crafts, although there are also access points for canoes and kayaks within the main section of the park, as well. Many big and small boats put in here at Dinah's Landing where they can enjoy the wide Pamlico River and even head down to the Sound and the ocean.

With so much water abounding, fishing in the creeks or river is popular at the park. Anglers will find both fresh and saltwater fish including largemouth bass, yellow and white perch, and bluegill. Waterbirds can be spotted along the river and creek, too, including mallards, ducks, Canadian geese, herons, and egrets. You may also see beavers, otters, turtles, raccoons, and muskrats in or near the water as well as water snakes.

Returning to the Main Road and following to its end leads past a group camp area to one of the park's most popular locations, especially in summer. A grassy picnic lawn spreads out under the trees near the parking area at the end of Main Road and a sidewalk leads down to the broad, sandy swim beach on the Pamlico River. This is a beautiful spot with picnic tables and a wide beach for water fun and relaxation. The views across the broad Pamlico River are gorgeous and on the warm June day we visited, we found the beach, for a mile in both directions, filled with families enjoying the day, the sun, and the water. Many had set up tents or gathered chairs along the river banks and we

were a little envious of the good time everyone was obviously enjoying. The half-mile Live Oak Trail winds along the river here with live oaks draped in Spanish moss along its way—a lovely sight. The 1-mile Mallard Creek Loop Trail links into the Live Oak Trail and winds to Mallard Creek and back again.

Goose Creek is a memorable park that will make you yearn to visit again to enjoy trails or spots you missed the first time, to swim or boat, hike or walk, or simply sit on a bench and gaze out on the beauty of the river or creeks.

Fort Raleigh National Historic Site

Tidewater Region - Dare County

Park Address: 1401 National Park Drive, Manteo, NC 27854

Park Size: 355 acres   Month Visited: June

Directions: From Interstate-95 at Rocky Mount, take Hwy 64 East. Pass through Washington and continue on 64 into Manteo. Turn left on Hwy 64 and follow to the northern end of the island. Turn right on Fort Raleigh Road and follow signs to the parking area and visitor center.

Park Description:

      Fort Raleigh, a National Historic Site and Park, is found at the north end of Roanoke Island in Manteo. Tucked away from the Atlantic Ocean on a long strip of land between Roanoke and Croatan Sounds, the first English settlers probably envisioned it an ideal place to create a colony in the New World. The national site now preserves and tells the story of this first English colony, Fort Raleigh, and the history of later settlements and Civil War battles. The park is beautifully maintained and it is entertaining, as well as educational, to explore the park's grounds and to learn about the rich history of the area.

      The best place to begin an exploration of Fort Raleigh is at the Lindsay

Warren Visitor Center. Within the center you can get a brochure with a walking map, enjoy the exhibits and museum room, and look at books, media and other items for sale in the park store. You can also watch an excellent 17-minute film about the park's history, shown every half hour in the center's theater. In addition, park rangers give regular guided tours and talks for visitors and a tour was beginning just as we visited the park.

To begin exploring the park grounds, stop to see the Freedmen's Colony Monument at the end of the visitor center plaza. To the right of the monument a paved walkway leads back to the reconstructed earthen remains of the fort with markers and signs along the way to tell the history. Along the trail to the fort you will also see the 1896 Monument, telling about the first colony to settle at Roanoke. Other trails in the park are the 0.4-mile Thomas Harriot Trail looping out and back to the Albemarle Sound, starting past the fort, and the 2.4-miles Freedom Trail beginning at the Elizabethan Gardens. Walkers and bikers enjoy the trails throughout the park.

Beyond the fort remains, the main trail leads to its end at the Waterside Theatre that shows *The Lost Colony* show. In 2022, the outdoor drama celebrated its 85th year of depicting the Lost Colony's story to visitors from all over the world. The colorful show begins nightly in season at the park and over 4.5 million people have enjoyed the performances in a beautiful setting. *The Lost Colony* has been awarded a Tony Honor for Excellence in Theatre, and it is an entertaining, well-produced event with mu-

19

sic, song, rich period costumes, dancing, and a cast of over 60 people. Information about show times and tickets can be found on *The Lost Colony* website.

Another side trail in the park leads to the Lost Colony Administrative building and to the Elizabethan Gardens. In 1953, the Garden Club of North Carolina decided to create an "English Pleasure Garden" to commemorate Sir Walter Raleigh and Queen Elizabeth's "Lost Colony." They leased the site for the garden beside Fort Raleigh National Historic Site and commissioned landscape architects to create a lovely two-acre garden. Over time statuary, fountains, a sundial, benches, and lovely walkways were created around the grounds. The garden trails wind by a sunken garden, an overlook terrace, a butterfly garden, through magnolia and camelia walks, and past other points of interest. It takes about an hour to walk through the garden and more information and ticket prices can be found on the Elizabethan Gardens website.

History Note:

Sir Walter Raleigh (1552-1618) was a favorite courtier of Queen Elizabeth I. As well as being an early adventurer and explorer, he was a statesman, soldier, and writer, and he held vast estates and properties in England. In 1584, he funded a voyage to bring 117 English men, women, and children to establish a permanent English colony in the New World. Raleigh's five ships and its settlers sailed from Plymouth in 1585, under the leadership of Colony Governor John White. In 1587, the first child was born at the new colony, to John White's daughter Eleanor and her husband Ananias Dare, and named Virginia. The colonists settled on Roanoke Island and soon faced a difficult time. John White sailed back to England shortly after Virginia Dare's birth to try to bring back more supplies and more reinforce-

ments to the settlement. Multiple problems ensued in returning, but three years later John White finally gained passage to return, reaching Roanoke in 1590. Three years had passed and White found no trace of the colony on his return. The only clue was the word "Croatoan" carved on a post, an early name for Hatteras Island nearby. To this day no one is sure what happened to this colony of English settlers and thus it came to be known as "The Lost Colony." Historians have suggested the colonists died from disease, famine, a hurricane, or were killed by hostile Spaniards or Native Americans, but though archeologists still search for the answers, none have been found.

Jockey's Ridge State Park

Tidewater Region - Dare County
Park Address: 300 West Carolista Drive, Nags Head, SC 27959
Park Size: 427 acres   Month Visited: June
Directions: From I-95 at Rocky Mount, take Hwy 64 East. Pass through Washington and continue on 64 into and through Manteo. Turn left on Hwy 158/Croatan Hwy, and follow to Milepost 12 and Carolista Drive on the left, the entrance to the park.

Park Description:

Established in 1975, this is an interesting park of high sand dunes, sweeping views of the Atlantic Ocean and Roanoke Sound, and winding trails through sand hills and maritime forest. Carolista Drive leads directly to the main parking lot and the park's large Visitor Center. The center, recently remodeled, has wide front and back porches and inside the center you can pick up a park map, get information about the park, and enjoy interactive exhibits and a museum about the cultural and natural history of the dunes and coast. To the left of the center a short shady trail leads to a designated picnic area with open tables and eight covered picnic shelters.

Next to the visitor center you'll see a colorful hang glider display beside a pathway winding down to the hang-gliding school. Dune hang gliding lessons are given by the school staff, providing opportunities to try out this air-borne sport while at the park. Windsurfing on the Roanoke Sound is also popular as is dune sledding on a surf board in designated areas. Another popular sport at Jockey's Ridge is kite flying, and the day we visited the park one of the Kite Festivals, often held at the park, was taking place. We enjoyed seeing all the large colorful kites, in a multitude of shapes and sizes, floating in the breezes above the dunes. The year-round winds, often blowing 10-15 miles an hour, make Jockey's Ridge ideal for these sports.

Jockey's Ridge State Park is the most popular park in the North Carolina system and on busy days you may find a lot of visitors at the site. The park has the tallest active sand dune in the eastern United States and ev-

eryone needs to take a walk out to see the high dunes at this park. The dunes area is accessed by a path and 360-ft long boardwalk that leads out to a high observation deck looking toward the dunes to either side. A long stairway leads down from the observation deck to the trails winding over and across the dunes. Wear good closed shoes, like canvas shoes, instead of flip flops or sandals, to walk on the sand trails, as the sand gets very hot, often 30 degrees hotter than the daily temperature. Since there is no shade, it is also a good idea to wear sunscreen and to take water with you to explore the dunes trails.

To the left of the Observation Deck the approximately 1-mile Ridge Trail winds below the deck and then

up and across the high park dunes. On a long ridge here, a crowd was gathered with tents, chairs, and kites for the ongoing Kite Festival. The 1.5-mile Tracks in the Sand Trail leads to the right of the observation deck across the dunes and then back to the Roanoke Sound. There are interesting interpretive stations on this trail telling about the sights along the way.

The largest sand dune at Jockey's Ridge is 80-100 feet tall and the ridge of dunes is made up of almost 30 million tons of sand. The dunes, thought to be 7,000 years old, are active, often shifting and changing. With such high dunes along the coast, a lot of shipwrecks happened here in early history and the "wild horses" of the Outer Banks are believed to have come from these ships. In the 1800s, a grand hotel was built at the base of one of the dune ridges, but soon the sand of the ridges began to cover the hotel until it was eventually buried and closed. The dunes swallowed up a mini golf course in the past, too.

The backside of Jockey's Ridge State Park borders the Roanoke Sound. There is a sand swim beach here with a wooden boardwalk leading from the

parking lot down to the beach. On a warm summer's day, the shoreline is crowded with families and visitors boating, swimming, and enjoying the day by the water. The park's other trail, the Soundside Trail, a self-guided nature trail, begins out of the free parking lot here to loop for a mile around through the maritime forest and along the Sound.

Jockey's Ridge is a memorable park you won't soon forget. Although the park does not have a designated campground, there are several large campgrounds nearby. And across the highway is a public beach access point on the Atlantic Ocean at Hollowell Street. Visitors can park here and walk across a boardwalk to enjoy a stroll by the ocean before leaving.

Pettigrew State Park

Tidewater Region - Washington County
Park Address: 2252 Lake Shore Road, Creswell, NC 27928
Park Size: 5,951 acres   Month Visited: June
Directions: From Hwy 64 E, take Exit 558 at Creswell. Follow Alligood Road/6th Street into Creswell. Turn left on Main. Follow across the Scupernong River on Spruill Bridge Rd to right on Thirty Foot Canal Rd. Right on Lake Shore Rd to Park entrance.

Park Description:

      The main section of Pettigrew State Park is found along the northeast shore of 16,600-acre Phelps Lake, the second largest natural lake in North Carolina. In the main park area is the visitor center, a small campground, a picnic grounds, several walking trails, a swim area on the lake, and a boat ramp. A second boat access point and a long fishing pier can be found off Shore Road at Cypress Point on the west end of the lake, with a third at Pocosin Natural Area, on the lake's south side, where you'll also find a nature trail and an observation overlook.

      In the main park area by the visitor center you can stroll over to a nice picnic area with tables and shelters tucked under giant cypress trees. The visitor center was not open on the Saturday we visited so we were glad we'd brought our own map to help us find our way around. A loop road next to the picnic area

leads to the park's family campground with 13 campsites. The sites, with tables and grills, are big enough for small RVs but there are no hookups or a dump station.

This park is rich in history and a part of Pettigrew's acreage includes the lands of two former Antebellum plantations, Bonarva and Somerset Place. The park is named for Confederate General James Pettigrew who owned Bonarva and was mortally wounded at Gettysburg. A trail from the end of the campground, the Bee Tree Trail, leads to Somerset Plantation, now called Somerset Place State Historic Site, and then on to the land where Bonarva once stood.

In the 1700s, Josiah Collins and associates bought 100,000 acres of land, including Phelps Lake. He brought enslaved men and women to help drain the land, dig out a six-mile canal, and built over a time a prosperous plantation. Josiah Collins bought out his partners and in 1819 his son inherited the land. The family actually lived in Edenton, North Carolina, at some distance from the plantation but Josiah II, and then his son Josiah III, continued to grow and develop

the property. By the mid 1800s the plantation had 50 structures, barns, stables, slave houses, a smokehouse, storehouses, a laundry, dairy, a sailing house and a chapel. Josiah III and his wife Mary began spending more time at the plantation after they inherited and in 1830 they built the large, two-storied Collins Mansion, which still stands.

Somerset Plantation did not continue after the Civil War and later had to be sold. In 1939, the state of North Carolina obtained a lease on the land, incorporating it into Pettigrew State Park when it opened, and in 1945 the state bought Somerset and have continued restoration efforts to bring alive to visitors what a large Antebellum plantation was once like. It feels like stepping back in time to walk around the Somerset historic site and visitors can take informative tours of the site for a very modest fee.

Bonarva Plantation did not survive after the war either and the original plantation house no longer stands, but you can walk further down the Bee Tree Trail, past Somerset, and take a side trail to the Bonarva family cemetery. The General's gravestone has

a cross on the top of it. To extend your hike, walk on to the end of the Bee Tree Trail to the canal and a fine overlook across the lake.

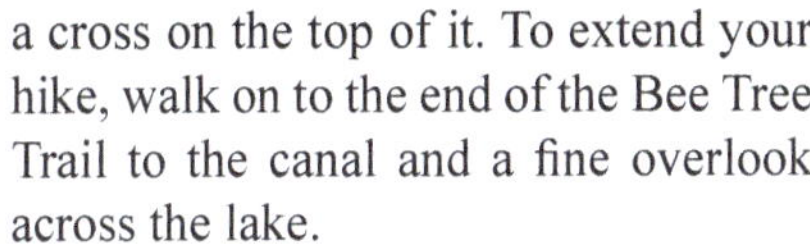

Back at the visitor center, we drove to the boat ramp to enjoy more views of Phelps Lake and to walk out on the long pier there. Phelps Lake is believed to be over 38,000 years old and its origin is still a mystery. The remains of old canoes, created by the Algonquin Indians, have been found in the lake and you can see two of those at the park's visitor center. The waters of Phelps Lake are surprisingly clear and clean, and shallow, with the lake's average depth only 4.5 to 9 feet deep.

Boating and swimming are popular at the lake. On the road to the ramp the Lake Shore Trail leads down a boardwalk trail through the woods to a fine swim pier with ladders. The lake is wonderful for kayak, canoe, and shallow bottom boating fun and for fishing. The lake is especially known for bass, yellow perch, catfish, and pickerel. This lovely park on a gorgeous lake offers unexpected pleasures in a beautiful setting and if you have time for a longer 6-mile roundtrip hike, the Moccasin Trail winds from behind the center, across a 350-foot boardwalk through a cypress swamp to a spectacular view across the lake to end your day.

Wright Brothers National Memorial

Tidewater Region - Dare County
Park Address: 1000 Croatan Hwy, Kill Devil Hills, NC 27959
Park Size: 428 acres   Month Visited: June
Directions: From I-95, take Hwy 64 East. Pass through Washington and continue on 64 through Manteo. Turn left on Hwy 158/ Croatan Hwy, and follow to Milepost 7.5 in Kill Devil Hills and turn left into park entrance.

Park Description:

This national memorial site, commemorating Orville and Wilbur Wright's first successful flight of a power-driven air machine, was transferred from the War Department to the National Park Service in 1933. The memorial site includes a visitor center and museum, the first flight airstrip and flight markers, a reconstructed hanger and workshop, and several rock monuments, the most prominent of which sits on Kill Devil Hills. There is a fee to enter this park so check the park's website before visiting for details. At the time we visited, cash payments would not be accepted, only credit card payments.

From the parking lot, begin your visit at the modern visitor center. The center features interactive exhibits, early plane replicas, a full-scale replica of the brothers' 1903 flyer, explanations about how planes are built and are able to fly, photos of early aircrafts, and facts about the Wright Brothers' lives. The center is a fascinating place to visit in itself.

Outside the center, visitors can walk around the grounds where the Wright Brothers built and worked on their early airplanes and made their first successful flight. Paved walkways wind around to a reconstructed airplane hanger and workshop, with quarters you can peek into, and an interpretive sign beside it with explanations. The large First Flight boulder sits beside the hanger and by the start of the long airstrip with flight markers along its way.

From the visitor center a long walkway leads to the Wright Brothers Monument at the top of Kill Devil Hills. The 60-foot-high granite monument is impressive and from the top of the hill, or from the observation platform at the top of the monument, visitors can see across the dunes to the Albemarle Sound and to the ocean. The monument's inscription reads: "In commemoration of the conquest of the air by the brothers Wilbur and Orville Wright."

History Note:
Orville Wright (1871-1948) and Wilbur Wright (1867-1912) were brothers from Dayton, Ohio. Always entrepreneurs in spirit, and encouraged in creative and intellectual interests by their parents, they owned a print shop and a bicycle shop before beginning to experiment on gliders for air travel in 1899. After searching for a site, the brothers learned that Kitty Hawk, North Carolina, had the consistent wind needed for a first flight. The brothers moved there, living and working on their first planes. Their first successful flight was made on December 17, 1903, for twelve seconds at eight feet in the air. Both brothers flew their airplane a couple of times on that day and their flights made headlines and paved the way for aviation to come. In the 1920s, the U.S. government formally acknowledged the brothers as innovators, and in 1927, President Coolidge signed a bill to have a national memorial built in Kill Devil Hills.

Cape Hatteras National Seashore

Tidewater Region- Dare County
Park Address: 1401 National Park Drive, Manteo, NC 27854
Park Size: 24,470 acres   Month Visited: June
Directions: From I-95 at Rocky Mount, take Hwy 64 East and over bridge into Manteo. Follow Hwy 64 staying right to cross second bridge, turning south on NC Hwy 12.

Park Description:

The Cape Hatteras National Seashore follows Hwy 12 from north to south, from Bodie Island to Ocracoke Island, along a long, windswept roadway on the Atlantic Coast. The national seashore, established in 1953, contains 70 miles of unbroken ocean front and about 28,500 acres. It is approximately 45 miles from Bodie Island on the north to Hatteras Island on the south and about an hour's drive, a nice day's exploration journey. If you continue to Ocracoke Island, add in two hours for the ferry over and back, and another hour to explore the island there.

As you drive down Hwy 12 into the national seashore, you will soon leave behind the commercialism of the northern Outer Banks. Our first stop in the park was at the Bodie Island Lighthouse. The Bodie Island Light, still operative today, sits on the north side of the Oregon Inlet a few miles south of the entrance

to the National Seashore. Here you can visit the old keeper's house and visitor center and then follow the long boardwalk trail out to an observation deck and to the lighthouse. If you wish, you can climb to the top of the lighthouse for a fee to see the views. At night, ships at sea can see the light from the light-house for 20 miles off shore.

Near the Bodie Island lighthouse is Coquina Beach,

one of the park's many public beaches on the ocean with a bathhouse, restrooms, and a broad expanse of white beach. Not far from the beach is the Oregon Inlet Campground, one of four park campgrounds. Across the road from the camp-ground is the Oregon Inlet Marina and Coast Guard Station next to the 2.8-miles Marc Basnight Bridge to Pea Island. Boats of all sizes put in and out of the marina daily to head out to fish or enjoy time on the water. The Oregon Inlet Fishing Center is the largest and most modern commercial charter fishing marina on the eastern seaboard, also providing boat ramps, boat rentals, fuel sales, fish cleaning and packaging, and other services.

After crossing the bridge beyond the marina, you enter the Pea Island National Wildlife Refuge. The 5,834-acre refuge, extending from the Oregon In-

let to Rodanthe, was established to provide and protect the habitat of waterfowl, migratory birds, and other wildlife. The Outer Banks boasts over 365 species of wading and shore birds that live or nest here as do mammals like river otters and loggerhead sea turtles. We really enjoyed stopping at the Refuge Visitor Center to see the interesting exhibits there and to learn more about their work. Within the refuge are public beaches and kayak access points to enjoy, along with nature trails, observation trails, and interpretive kiosks about wildlife you might see.

A busy commercial area, the "Tri-Villages" of Rodanthe, Waves, and Salvo, follows the refuge. You can stop to pick up lunch at one of the cute cafes or restaurants, poke in quaint shops, or enjoy time at the Rodanthe public beach access where a boardwalk leads to a covered gazebo and the ocean. Overnight or vacation rentals are abundant here and the beaches, especially at the "S Curves," are popular for surfing. The Pamlico Sound draws kiteboarders, windsurfers, and paddle boarders alike at the Salvo Day Area. All these small villages developed in the 1800s, isolated and remote then, and the area is rich with history. You can visit the Chicamacomico Life-Saving Station Historic Site and museum at Rodanthe to learn tales of heroism about the men of this coastal military branch who saved many lives from shipwrecked vessels along the Outer Banks shores. This entire coastal area is often called "The Graveyard of the Atlantic."

Beyond Salvo, half way between the "Tri-Villages" and Avon, look for Beach Access Ramp 27 and pull over and stop where you see a big sign at the parking area by the boardwalk titled "Rescue of the Priscilla." The sign tells the story of a life-saving rescue that occurred at this spot in 1899 when Rasmus

Midgett heroically rescued ten men from the wrecked ship Priscilla in a harsh storm. This is a nice beach spot, too, away from the busy towns nearby.

In Avon, thought of as the "Center of Hatteras Island," you'll find a well-developed and more populous community with many restaurants, gift shops, a large grocery store, a mini-golf course and other amenities, as well as a multitude of beach house rentals. An attraction to look for in Avon is the Avon Fishing Pier, established in 1963 and a local landmark. For a small fee you can walk out on the 600-foot wooden pier to enjoy the ocean views or pay to fish for the day from the pier. Anglers catch drum, bluefish, mullet, and other fish, and on the Fourth of July, the pier is the launching point for the Annual 4th of July Fireworks display.

Our journey on this trip ended at Hatteras. In Buxton we stopped to see the Cape Hatteras Lighthouse, Light Station and Visitor Center Museum. The Cape Hatteras Lighthouse, first lit in 1803, is the tallest lighthouse in the United States, over 198 feet from the ground to the rod. Visitors can climb up the winding staircase to the top of the lighthouse for fantastic views, if they are willing to walk up over 250 steps. Just beyond the lighthouse is the Frisco Campground, a large, uncrowded campground with 127 spacious sites, bathhouses and several gorgeous beach accesses that wind down pretty trails and over boardwalks to the beach.

At the island's end at Hatteras, a ferry can take you on to Ocracoke for more explorations and to see the Ocracoke Lighthouse, the third of the park's lighthouses. The ferry over and back to Ocracoke is free but the waits can be long. Points to see are Okracoke Village, the shops and galleries around Silver Lake Harbor, and historic points on the island.

Cape Lookout National Seashore

Tidewater Region - Carteret County
Park Address: 1800 Island Road, Harkers Island, NC 28531
Park Size: 28,000 acres   Month Visited: June
Directions: From Hwy 17 below New Bern, exit onto Hwy 70 south. Turn left on Hwy 101 at Havelock. Continue left on Laurel Rd and after appx. 2 miles turn right on Merriman Rd. Turn left on Hwy 70. Follow to Otway and right on Harkers Island Rd. Cross bridge to island and follow Island Rd to visitor center.

Park Description:

The Cape Lookout National Seashore Park is not accessible directly by road in your car but only accessible by ferries. The long stretch of seashore from the North Core to the South Core of the park is windswept, remote, isolated, and basically undeveloped. Each section of the long 56-mile stretch of seashore has its own unique charm as does the visitor center.

The main visitor center for Cape Lookout is on Harkers Island. From there a ferry takes passengers over to the Light Station on South Core. We were charmed with the small, laid-back picturesque town of Harkers Island and with the beautiful Cape Lookout visitor center at the end of the island with sweeping vistas out over the water.

In the visitor center is an information desk, gift shop, and beautiful interactive displays about the national seashore, island ecology, the lighthouse, the Shackleford horses, Portsmouth Village and more. The center has a great Kids Corner, enjoyed by kids and adults, and a fine park film. Outdoor signs also tell about the National Seashore and a big anchor in front of the center offers a great spot for a memory photo. Other small visitor centers can be found at Beaufort, Cape Lookout Light Station, on Great Island and on Long Point, and at Portsmouth—but this is the largest and the park headquarters.

Across from the visitor center is the Shell Point picnic area with nice shelters and tables. The grassy area looks across the waters of the sound toward Shackleford Island, with views to the Cape Lookout lighthouse in the distance. There is a kayak and canoe access point at Shell Point and we enjoyed talking with a couple who had kayaked to Cape Lookout and camped overnight on the beach. There are no campgrounds on the seashore, but primitive camping is allowed, with a "take-all-in-take-all-out" understanding.

There are no designated hiking trails on the barrier islands, either, but there are two trails on Harkers Island, near the Visitor Center. The Soundside Loop Trail winds for approximately one mile from behind the visitor center through the maritime forest to the marsh. Also from the center you can hike the 1.3 mile Willow Pond Trail, that circles a pond behind the beautiful Core Sound Waterfowl Museum and Heritage Center. The museum, in partnership with the Cape Lookout National Seashore, is an interesting facility to visit, and free to the public. It contains museum rooms, historic collections, galleries, exhibits, and a lovely gift shop. Many of the exhibits preserve the past memories of people who grew up, lived and worked on Harkers Island or on a part of the National Seashore.

To make an extended visit to any part of the Cape Lookout National Seashore will take some dedicated planning and a large block of time. We didn't have the time to visit the seashore on this trip but if you have time on your visit, plan to take the 20-30-minute ferry to the Cape Lookout Lighthouse and village. There is a ferry pick up pavilion in front of the visitor center and the ferry runs every hour with wait stations at both ends. The ferry route travels past Shackleford Island, where you may get a glimpse of

the wild horses who make their home there. At the Lighthouse dock, a long boardwalk leads to the black-and-white diamond patterned Cape Lookout Lighthouse. The lighthouse was first built in 1812 but later replaced with a taller 163-foot structure in 1859. Visitors can climb the 207 steps to the top of the lighthouse for a small fee. Cape Lookout Lighthouse is still operating and its light reaches 19 miles out to sea at night. Beside the visitor center, you can also visit the old Keeper's House and the old Coast Guard house. In the early 1900s there were still residents here at the Cape Lookout Village with a post office and a small school but by 1921, after several bad hurricanes, few remained. Now mainly vacationers come to see the light and walk the trails and boardwalks down to the ocean. Al-

though there are restrooms at the lighthouse, there are no shops on the island, so be sure to take everything you might need with you—water, sun lotion, sunglasses, insect repellent, and beach necessities if you expect to stay for a time. The ferry will pick you up and take you back to the visitor center after your visit.

Further up the national seashore, visitors can also take a ferry, which allows vehicles, over to Great Island where there are rental cabins, restrooms, and a bathhouse. Further up on another of the national seashore islands, a ferry leads to more cabins at Long Point. A 45-minute ferry also leads from Okracoke Island to Portsmouth at the far northern end of the seashore. Portsmouth was once a fishing village, and several historic homes and buildings remain that you can explore. Visiting any part of the Cape Lookout National Seashore is a unique adventure, like stepping back to a time before all the common amenities we take for granted came to be.

Carolina Beach State Park

Tidewater Region - New Hanover County
Park Address: 1010 State Park Road, Carolina Beach, NC 28428
Park Size: 761 acres   Month Visited: June
Directions: From Wilmington, NC take Hwy 421 South and follow across Snow's Cat Bridge over the intercoastal waterway. Turn right at the second stop-light onto Dow Road. Follow signs to park entrance and turn right on State Park Road.

Park Description:

Carolina Beach State Park, established in 1969, is in a busy location below Wilmington, NC, but it's an amazingly quiet and lovely park tucked away from the main highway on the Cape Fear River. As a plus, the small park is not far from a long row of popular beaches facing the Atlantic Ocean, too. The park sits in a wedge of land on Pleasure Island with its back side facing the Cape Fear River and its north side facing the Snow's Cut Intracoastal Waterway. You can imagine with all that water access, that this is a great park for boating and fishing of all kinds. Visitors will also find nice camping areas, a full -size marina, two boat ramps, and nine scenic hiking trails twining through the park's grounds.

The visitor center features a wide variety of exhibits. These displays and exhibits allow visitors a deeper look at the park's ecology and the interesting

plants and wildlife they might see. Displays also tell the history of the park and general area and give facts about animal habitats. Carolina Beach State Park is one of the few parks where you can actually see five different carnivorous plants. Videos and exhibits introduce visitors to these plants which include pitcher plants, butterworts, sundews, and the well-known Venus Fly Trap. On the back deck of the

visitor center, the rangers have even created a small garden of some of these plants in case visitors miss seeing them while at the park.

Beside the visitor center the Campground Trail begins, winding in one direction to the main campground and in the other direction to connect with the 0.75-mile Swamp Trail and the park's two group camps. A map provided at the visitor center shows the location of and describes all nine trails in the park. Rangers offer scheduled hiking events you might enjoy to acquaint visitors with the park's interesting diversity of plants and birds. For any hike spritzing with insect repellent is highly recommended, as many of the trails wind through the swamp

forests and brackish marshes, across long boardwalks, and by lowland ponds. These shallow limesink ponds, named the Cypress Pond, Lily Pond, and Grass Pond, are all located not far off the Campground Trail on the early portion of the 3-mile-long Sugarloaf Trail. The Sugarloaf Trail travels back to the Cape Fear River and to the high 50-foot-tall Sugarloaf Dune, once an important navigational and miliary marker. There are several other nice overlooks across the Cape Fear River on this trail, too, and on the 0.25-mile Oak Toe Trail that connects to it.

Travelers will find the park campground a short distance up the road from the visitor center. There are 83 family campsites on the campground's two loop roads, ten with full hookups for large RVs, four with electric and water hook-up only, and sixty-nine with no hookups, perfect for tent camping. Between the two loop roads are also four camper cabins that can be rented from the park. Each cabin has a double bed and bunks to sleep six in two rooms with a heat-and-air conditioning unit and electrical outlets. The campground has restrooms with hot showers located nearby and each campsite has a picnic table and grill or fire ring. No swimming is allowed at this park, but an access trail leads over to the Snow's Cut Trail along the Intracoastal Waterway, with nice spots to put in a kayak or canoe or to sit and fish on the bank. Trout, flounder and other fish can be caught off the river bank and from boats.

A short distance from the campground is a picnic area with picnic tables, restrooms, and grills and with more side trails leading to the banks of the Snow's Cut Intracoastal Waterway. Beyond the picnic area the park road ends at the ma-

rina. This is a beautiful spot with a 54-slip marina and a modern marina store that sells fuel, camping and fishing supplies, and offers restrooms, a laundry room, and a concession and snacks area. The marina has kayak, paddleboard, and canoe rentals and there are two nice public boat ramps.

A lovely trail winds from the marina to a fishing pier on the Cape Fear River. There are many quiet, scenic spots here, too, where visitors can sit on a bench and look out over the river. Beyond the marina, also, is an access point to the Sugarloaf Trail which leads to the Swamp Trail and other trails in the park.

On a side road before leaving the park, a road between the campground road and the visitor center winds to a parking area for the Flytrap Trail. This is a loop trail through a marshy, wetland and forested area that takes visitors to spots where they might see the Venus Fly-trap plants and other carnivorous plants. Watch for these along the edges of the pocosins, or wetland bogs with sandy soils and woody shrubs. In season, there are also many wildflowers along this trail. The Venus Fly Traps you might see here are only native to North and South Carolina and especially here at the Carolina Beach State Park. Please don't try to pick or dig up these plants as they are rare and threatened, and its illegal to harm or poach them.

Not far down the main highway from Carolina Beach State Park is Kure Beach. Kure Beach has a broad white sand beach on the Atlantic Ocean and a long 711-foot fishing pier that is the oldest fishing pier on the Atlantic coast. Carolina Beach Lake Park is another pretty spot to visit with its 11-acre fresh water lake with a children's playground, picnic shelters, and more. Plan to explore while you are in the area.

Fort Fisher State Historic Site

Tidewater Region - New Hanover County
Park Address: 1000 Loggerhead Road, Kure Beach, NC 28449
Park Size: 476 acres   Month Visited: June
Directions: From Wilmington NC take Hwy 421 South and follow through the towns of Carolina Beach and Kure Beach. Turn right into the historic site on Fort Fisher Blvd and after visiting return to Hwy 421 and turn left on Loggerhead Road to the Recreation area.

Park Description:

The properties of Fort Fisher State Historic Site and the Fort Fisher Recreation Area are within walking distance of each other on the tip of Pleasure Island below Wilmington. Both are governed by the state of North Carolina so it would be a shame not to visit both while in the area. The Historic site has remains of an old Confederate fort, a fine museum, and walking trails, and the recreation area has miles of beach to enjoy, a trail through the marsh, and the North Carolina Aquarium. Neither park area offers camping but several campgrounds can be found not far to the north, as well as an abundance of restaurants, shops, and entertainments.

We stopped to first visit and explore the Fort Fisher State Historic Site. The history of this park is fascinating and the visitor center and museum have wonderful exhibits and displays that explain the signifi-cance of the fort. You can also watch an excellent ten-minute audiovisual program that brings the fort's history to life in film. Tours are given regularly and we also enjoyed snapping a photo of one of the rangers in costume.

Fort Fisher, called the "Gibral-ter of the South," was the last fortress protecting the ports of the Confederacy in the final months of the War Between the States. It took two intense battles to conquer it. The first, in 1864, failed but in the second, in 1865, Union forces successfully defeated the Confederates and took over the fort. The battle has been called the "largest amphibious at-tack by US forces" before Normandy Beach during World War II, and Fort Fisher's defeat helped to seal the fate of the Confederacy.

In the quarter mile tour around the fort's grounds, you'll see the re-maining earthernware fortifications of the fort, a restored gun emplacement on top of one of the batteries, an under-ground bunker, and cannons of several types, like the Armstrong Cannon. The trail winds back to cross a boardwalk along the Cape Fear River with obser-vation areas along the way and with signs explaining the sights you see. An army battalion was storming the hill the day we visited, too, adding to the pleasure of our visit.

Across from the visitor center and museum is a paved walkway along the Cape Fear River, with a huge rocky

barrier by the beach to try to stop ongoing erosion. There are picnic tables and benches under the trees and one couple had strung up a hammock for a nap in the breeze. At the end of the walkway is a covered pavilion offering fine views down the shore.

As you leave the historic site, and start south on Hwy 421, watch for a side road to the left, called the Battle Acre Road. You can stop there to see the tall white Confederate Monument bearing the names of Confederate soldiers who lost their lives at the Battle of Fort Fisher.

The next road to the left, Loggerhead Road, winds down to the Fort Fisher State Recreation Area. Here you'll find another nice visitor center with exhibits to enjoy, a pathway and boardwalk leading to a picnic area and on to a beautiful stretch of white, sandy beach. This is a designated swim area and in the busy months of the year a lifeguard is on duty. A beach walk can take you further along the nearly seven miles of pristine, uncommercial beach. For a fee, visitors with strong, four-wheel vehicles can purchase a permit to drive down the sands to set up a beach camp or fishing camp for the day. No ATVs or UTVs are allowed access and

caution needs to be taken with no paved roads or facilities on this deserted beach stretch. Hurricane Floyd in 1999 partly connected Fort Fisher to Bald Head Island to the south, and long-distance hikers can now hike about twenty miles roundtrip

46

to Bald Head and back. However, it's a harsh trail with no shade cover, no facilities, and often difficult soft sand conditions. For the average visitor, a stroll or walk for a mile or two along Fort Fisher's beautiful beach is enough.

Another hike of interest is the park's Basin Trail. It begins at a trail-head near the center, and crosses a marshland area on a long boardwalk or two before winding past an old World War II bunker. The trail ends at an over-look on the Cape Fear River and nearby you'll find the partial earthernworks of Battery Buchanan and another Con-federate marker. On your way down or back on the Basin Trail, be sure to stop to look more closely at the old bunker. It was once the home of the hermit Rob-ert Harrill and you will find his grave marker nearby, too. In 1955, Robert, at 62, left a troubled life, some say escap-ing from a mental institution, and hitch-hiked for 260 miles to Carolina Beach. He then walked to Fort Fisher and dis-covered the abandoned World War II artillery bunker. Turning his back on the world, Robert Harrill lived the next 17 years there, becoming a local legend

over time. People donated money and goods to him and enjoyed visiting him and hearing his homespun wisdom and ideas about life.

Before you leave Fort Fisher, take a drive down to the end of Hwy 421 to see the Fort Fisher Ferry terminal and the Federal Point Boat Launch. At the road's end, you can walk down to the Rocks at Fort Fisher and on the long rock jetty and perhaps watch the sunset over the water.

Fort Macon State Park

Tidewater Region - Carteret County
Park Address: 2300 E. Fort Macon Rd, Atlantic Beach, NC 28512
Park Size: 424 acres   Month Visited: June
Directions: From I-95, take US Hwy 70 East to Morehead City and turn south on Atlantic Beach. Cross the bridge to Atlantic Beach and turn left on NC 58 to end of island and into the state park.

Park Description:

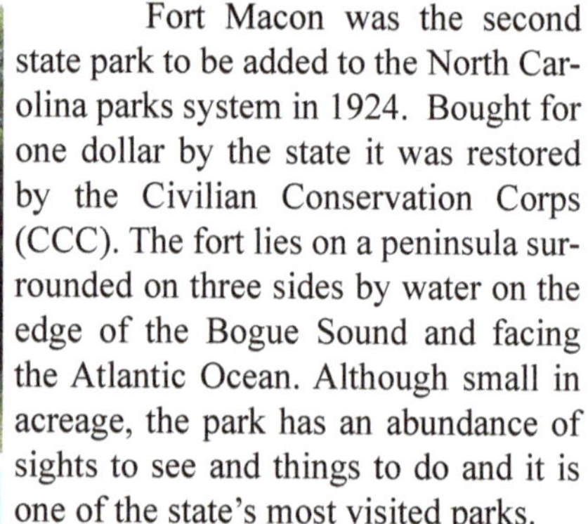

Fort Macon was the second state park to be added to the North Carolina parks system in 1924. Bought for one dollar by the state it was restored by the Civilian Conservation Corps (CCC). The fort lies on a peninsula surrounded on three sides by water on the edge of the Bogue Sound and facing the Atlantic Ocean. Although small in acreage, the park has an abundance of sights to see and things to do and it is one of the state's most visited parks.

The fort is the centerpiece of the park and Fort Macon is larger than any other U.S. fort, an impressive five-sided walled structure of brick and stone. Around the fort's inner walls are a moat and additional walls of protection. Over 2,370,800 bricks were used in building the entire fort and the outer walls are 4.5 feet thick. Off the spacious

inner court of the fort are 26 casement rooms, restored quarters, powder magazines, supply rooms, and more. Wide stairs rise up from the courtyard to the wall, where cannons are positioned. It's a treat to explore all around the interior and exterior of this large well-maintained fortress.

During earlier times in US history, in the 1700s-1800s, the danger of attacks from hostile nations and pirates was a real problem, and Beaufort and the surrounding area were often attacked. Leaders recognized that a fort for protection was needed. One fort was begun but not finished and then Fort Hampton was built, not far from the location of Fort Macon now, but it was washed away later by a hurricane.

North Carolina Senator Nathaniel Macon procured the funds to later build Fort Macon and it was garrisoned in 1834. When the Civil War began in 1861, North Carolina Confederate troops took the fort from Union forces. However, in 1862, in a huge battle, the Union army took the fort back again in a long siege and then retained control of the fort throughout the war. After the war Fort Macon was a federal prison from 1867 to 1876 and then used again for protection of the coastline during World War II.

The best place to learn about the fort and its history is at the park's big visitor center. Don't miss stopping there

to wander through the museum and the five different galleries displaying artifacts from the fort's history. You'll see there a scale model of the fort, a parade of past uniforms and old weapons, and you can enjoy watching a history video in the center's nice theater. At the center you can get a park map, pick up a tour guide brochure to use while visiting the fort, and learn about the other sections of the park as well. From the visitor center a paved walkway leads over to the fort and down a sloped sidewalk into Fort Macon's wide entry doors. Once inside you can wander through the fort at your leisure or stop to sit on a bench to rest for a few minutes. Free guided tours of the fort are also available, that you might want to take, and interesting reenactments and events are often held at the fort.

After touring Fort Macon, do take time to enjoy the other sections of the park's grounds. Several trails lead out from the visitor center parking area. One is the quarter mile Yarrows Loop, a short nature trail with informative signs along the way about plants and animals. A longer trail, the Elliott Coves Nature Trail, connects in a loop route for 3.2 miles through the maritime forest and marsh area. It crosses a boardwalk and over the main road to the beach swim area near the beginning of the park before winding back along the other side of the road to the visitor's center again. You

50

may spot herons or egrets on the trail, a variety of birds, and other wildlife. A path from the parking area also leads down to the jetty on the Beaufort Inlet beach and a 1.5-miles Beach Trail leads along the beach where you can see boats, birds, dolphins, and other wildlife and enjoy the sights along the ocean. A short distance down the road from the visitor center is a pull off parking area leading to the beach or across a long boardwalk to a scenic beach overlook pavilion. There are benches at the pavilion, providing a nice spot to sit and look out over the Atlantic.

Before leaving the park, stop at the beautiful bathhouse and swim area on the ocean. A large bathhouse with a concessions area, picnic tables, and a covered pavilion sit right off the parking lot. From the pavilion a long boardwalk walks out to the Atlantic to another covered pavilion with shaded benches and sweeping ocean views. A final boardwalk leads directly down to the beach where visitors can spend an afternoon enjoying the sun and ocean on a lovely non-commercial white sandy beach.

Fort Macon is known for good fishing both in the ocean and on the inlets around the park. Kayaking and canoeing are popular around the park's inlets and on the Bogue Sound and you will often see other water craft on the ocean, as well. There are no boat ramps in the park but Fort Macon Marina Ramp is not far up the road from the park. Also, only eight miles from Fort Macon is the Theodore Roosevelt Natural Area with a scenic nature trail. The North Carolina Aquarium is also there at Pine Knoll Shores, and Atlantic Beach has many hotels, restaurants, shops, and amusements for visitors to enjoy.

Hammocks Beach State Park

Tidewater Region - Onslow County
Park Address: 1572 State Rd 1511, Swansboro, NC 28584
Park Size: 1611 acres   Month Visited: June
Directions: From Hwy 17 from Jacksonville take Hwy 24 East
to Swansboro. Turn right on State Rd 1511 (Hammocks Beach
Road). Near the road's end, turn right into the park entrance.

Park Description:

Hammocks Beach is made up of the main park area near Swansboro, along with acreage on three islands off the mainland, all accessible only by boat or ferry. The main section of the park is centered around a large visitor center with views across the Intracoastal Waterway and Queens Creek. The park is a boaters' paradise and the well-known Bear Island on the Atlantic Ocean is popular for beach lovers. With so much accessible water, fishing is enjoyed from the bank and by boat, and anglers catch flounder, drum, trout, and bluefish.

At the park's visitor center you'll find a variety of exhibits and interpretive programs about the park and its interesting history. The center also offers diorama shows, videos, and has a long deck across the back of the building with benches and scenic views. Behind the center a paved walkway leads to picnic tables and a rental area for canoes, kayaks and paddleboards. Beyond the rental area, a paved walkway and boardwalk lead to a kayak and canoe launch area. The boat ramp for motor boats, fishing boats, and larger boats is at the Maintenance Area but there is also a pull-in boat dock by the boarding area for the park's ferry. A gated ramp leads to the dock and to the launch area for the ferry.

Near the ramp is a covered pavilion with picnic tables and beyond it is the start of the park's Live Oak Trail. The half-mile trail makes a loop into the forest and back. Off the trail are connections to the other park trails, which

lead deeper into the park's acreage. The 0.30-mile Evergreen Trail branches off the Live Oak Trail to connect to the one-mile Coastal Fringe Trail with three boardwalks in the marsh area. Branching off the Coastal Fringe Trail toward Queens Creek is the half mile Hickory Bluff Trail which rises up on the ridge for fine views across the water. All these park trails are relatively easy walks and provide an up-close look at the maritime forest, tidal marshes, shore birds, plants and animals at the park.

The Hammocks Beach ferry takes tourists to and from Bear Island on the ocean. The ferry runs daily in the summer, approximately every hour. Most visitors come with beach gear and umbrellas, or with light-weight tents, prepared to spend a day or afternoon at the ocean. A nice dock at Bear Island has a boardwalk ramp leading to a bathhouse, restrooms and a small concession stand. Trails lead through the dunes to a long, beautiful, 4-mile stretch of white sand beach on the Atlantic Ocean. There is a designated swim area on the beach and Bear Island is always private and peaceful. Primitive camping is allowed on the island and there are 14 campsites on the beach and inlet. Campers must register with the park and bring-in and take-out all their camping needs.

In addition to Bear Island and the mainland area, Hammocks Beach Park also owns 225-acre Higgins Island, an undeveloped maritime swamp forest, Dudley Island, a remote marshland island with some beach front, and little James Island to the northeast at the mouth of the White Oak River. Several paddle trails wind around and to these islands. A map showing each of the paddle trails with lengths and descriptions is available at the park office. This is a peaceful, quiet park with some memorable spots to visit and enjoy.

Moores Creek National Battlefield

Tidewater Region - Pender County
Park Address: 40 Patriots Hall Drive, Currie, NC 28435
Park Size: 88 acres   Month Visited: June
Directions: From I-40, driving south toward Wilmington, exit at Rocky Point onto Hwy 210 East. Follow Hwy 210 east, crossing Hwy 421, staying left on Hwy 210 toward Currie. Watch for Moores Creek Drive and entrance sign on the right.

Park Description:

This small national park honors and preserves the site of an important Revolutionary War battle fought in 1776. The park is open 9 am to 5 pm Wednesday through Sunday and closed on Mondays and Tuesdays and for all federal holidays. In the park is a fine visitor center with a museum, exhibits, and an excellent film about the battle fought at this historic site. Around the park grounds is an 0.7-mile walking trail leading to significant sites in the Moores Creek battle, and by monuments, artillery, and other points of interest. A side road leads to a picnic area, pavilion, a meeting facility, and amphitheater. The park also has a short 0.4-mile nature trail, the Tarhead Trail, that begins near the visitor center.

At the center, the park ranger, dressed in costume, shared the park's history with us and answered our questions. The park gives free tours and programs, and offers an excellent 10-minute park video titled "*In the Most Furi-*

ous Manner" which gives the history of the battle fought in a well-done and interesting presentation. Walking around to see the exhibits and displays in the museum also helps to bring the battle's time period to life. There is even an online "Virtual Tour" of the park you can watch in advance of your visit on the national park website. For teachers and students curriculum materials and field trips

can be accessed to help teach about the history of the 1700s and the Revolutionary War. Reenactments and other events are often held at the park, and historians give musket demonstrations.

The walk around the battlefield trail or History Trail, loops in part on a recycled rubber walkway from one side of the visitor center around through the battlefield grounds and back to end at the center again. Visitors can pick up a History Walking Tour brochure at the visitor center that explains each point along the route. Beginning on the left, one of the first monuments on the path is the tall white Women's Monument dedicated to Mary Slocum who fought in the battle and tended to the wounded. Other monuments follow along the trail, including the Moores Creek Loyalist Monument, the Grady Patriot Monument, and the tall,

tan Patriot Monument honoring the only Patriot soldier to die in the battle. Points of interest along the route mark the Old Stage Road taken by the Loyalists and the Bridge that proved so decisive in the battle. A long boardwalk leads across Moores Creek and through the swamp and marsh that provided additional protection to the Patriots. The History Trail loop is a pretty and easy trail to walk, winding by fields of savanna grass and a blackwater creek and marshland. You may hear warblers and other songbirds on your walk, frogs in the early evening, and in spring you may spot wildflowers scattered in the grasses.

As the trail curls to head back to the center a side trail branches over to the park's nice, shaded picnic area and pavilion and to the large Patriots Hall meeting room that can be rented for events. It also passes a small historic area with split rail fencing and an outdoor brick oven. Visitors can walk to this section of the park, as we did, or drive to it on Patriots Hall Drive. For a step back into history and a reminder of the War of Independence that Americans fought valiantly to gain their freedom, this is a great park to visit.

HISTORY NOTE:

In the American Revolutionary War (April 19, 1775 – September 3, 1783) American Patriots gained independence from Great Britain. The first skirmishes of the war began in the spring of 1775 in Lexington and Concord, Massachusetts, and by the summer American Patriots were in a full-scale war against Great Britain. In North Carolina, in the early part of the Revolution, divided loyalties for and against the British Crown still existed. A Loyalist group of wealthy merchants and landowners, Crown officials, and Scottish Highland immigrants were fighting against the American Patriots in their struggle to gain independence. In February of 1776, British troops

planned to march eastward to take Wilmington, NC, and points along the way. Patriots, learning of the plan, began to gather their forces for defense at strategic points. On February 26, 1776, the Loyalists sent a courier demanding the Patriots at Moores Creek to surrender. They refused and the Patriot troops moved camp to an earthernworks fort beyond the bridge to prepare for battle. They also par-

tially dismantled the bridge the Loyalists would have to cross. That night and into the early morning of February 27th, Loyalist troops walked right into an unexpected ambush, the Patriots opening fire and winning the battle in about thirty minutes. This battle was significant as it stopped the advance of British and Loyalist troops into the south, ended royal authority in North Carolina, and prompted the North Carolina delegates to the Continental Congress in Philadelphia to vote for independence. It was also the first significant victory for the Patriots in the American Revolution.

Jones Lake

COASTAL PLAIN REGION STATE PARK INDEX

Dismal Swamp State Park 60

Merchants Millpond State Park 62

Lumber River State Park 64

Lake Waccamaw State Park 66

Singletary Lake State Park 70

Jones Lake State Park 72

Cliffs of the Neuse State Park 76

Medoc Mountain State Park 80

Carvers Creek State Park 82

Raven Rock State Park 84

Weymouth Woods State Park 86

Coastal Plain Region
North Carolina PARKS

Merchants Millpond

Lake Wacccamaw

Dismal Swamp

Cliffs of the Neuse

Dismal Swamp State Park

Coastal Plain Region - Camden County
Park Address: 2294 US Hwy 17N, South Mills, NC 27979
Park Size: 14,432 acres   Month Visited: June
Directions: From Hwy 64, traveling east, turn left on Hwy 17 to Edenton. Continue on Hwy 17 to Elizabethton. Follow Hwy 17 north for about 20 miles to entrance to park on left.

Park Description:

The Dismal Swamp State Park links to the vast Great Dismal Swamp National Wildlife Refuge that sprawls over 750 square miles of land across the borders of North Carolina and Virginia. Lake Drummond lies in the middle of the densely forested wetland, and the entire area is considered a geological wonder. It was, and still is, a rugged and sometimes treacherous area where snakes, insects, and wild animals make their home. A large population of black bears live in the swamp along with a rich variety of birds and plants. The swamp, in its past history, was often a hiding place for fugitives and escaped slaves.

To aid in early transportation and to get lumber out of the swamp, the 22-miles Dismal Swamp Canal was built in the 1700s and 1800s. The canal connected the Chesapeake Bay in Virginia with the Albemarle Sound in North Carolina. The swamp's lands were later deeded to the Department of the Interior in 1974 for creation of the Great Dismal Swamp National Wildlife Refuge, and in 1989 the Dismal Swamp Welcome Center opened. In the early 2000s, a section of the swamp along Highway 17 in North Carolina, near the Welcome Center, became the Dismal Swamp State Park and opened to the public in 2008. In the

years that followed, trails and areas for the public to safely see parts of the Dismal Swamp were created. Today the public can learn about the swamp at the park visitor center and at the nearby North Carolina Welcome Center. They can also see the Canal, and walk or bike on some of the wetland park's many trails.

We enjoyed visiting both the State Park Visitor Center, across the canal bridge, as well as visiting the North Carolina Welcome Center, which shares the same parking lot. Visitors can easily walk from one side to the other. On the east side of the canal are picnic tables under the trees and a paved walkway alongside the canal. At the small canal office, visitors speak with and check in with a park ranger if they plan to hike any of the trails, before walking across the wide swing bridge into the park property. Inside the visitor center is an interesting museum of interactive exhibits, telling about the swamp, its history, its wildlife and more. Park rangers offer scheduled programs about the area and there is also a large gift shop in the center.

For those who want to see the park in more depth, there is a canoe/kayak launch area for water explorations and the park also offers a rich abundance of trails to hike or bike. Visitors can rent kayaks, canoes, or bicycles from the park. Most visitors walk some of the 2.2 miles Canal Road trail that follows from the visitor center alongside the canal. A half-mile Swamp Boardwalk trail, beginning behind the visitor center, provides a short loop walk into the wetlands and the 0.9-mile Supple Jack Trail leads to the remains of an old liquor still. Other old logging roadbeds have become trails that take visitors deeper into the wetlands, and the park has a map with their descriptions. Plan to bring proper shoes, clothing, and insect repellent for further ventures into the park's interior.

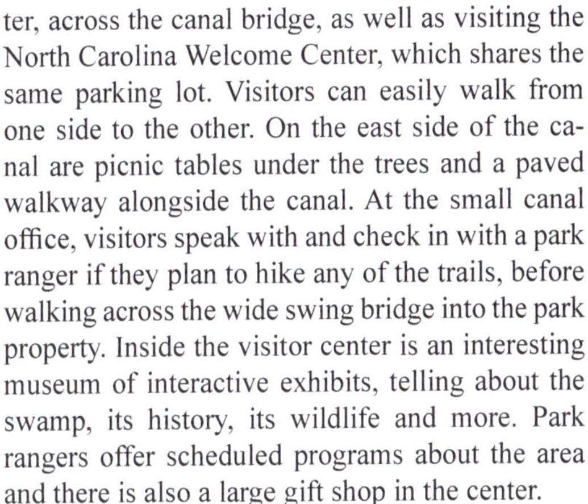

Merchants Millpond State Park

Coastal Plain Region- Gates County
Park Address: 176 Millpond Rd, Gatesville, NC 27938
Park Size: 3,520 acres   Month Visited: June
Directions: From Hwy 64, traveling east, turn left on Hwy 17 to Edenton. From Edenton, travel north on Hwy 32. At the intersection of 158 at Sunbury, turn left on Hwy 158 and follow to Mill Pond Road. Turn left on Mill Pond to park entrance on left.

Park Description:

This interesting small park spreads around a 700-acre millpond and the larger Lassiter Swamp. It has a small campground, walking trails, picnic areas, and access to the millpond and creeks for canoeing, kayaking, and fishing. The millpond is scenic with large bald cypress trees in and around the waters, along with tupelo gum, beech trees, and other hardwoods, many draped with Spanish moss. Research done by the U.S. Geological Survey of tree rings in the Lassiter Swamp show that many of the cypress trees there are at least 500 years old.

The visitor center is unexpectedly large and beautiful with a fine museum exhibit inside that we both enjoyed. The colorful exhibits tell about the park and area history, about the old gristmill that used to be on the pond, and about the wildlife you can expect to see around the park. Yellow cow lilies thrive on the millpond as does floating green duckweed in many areas. After a rain or in the evening, you may hear frogs of many types and see turtles, a variety of birds, otters, opossum, deer, raccoons, and beavers.

This is a great park for paddling and canoeing. Rental canoes are available at the park or you can bring your own canoe or kayak. There are several paddle trails near the visitor center plus a boat ramp on the south side of the park and several canoe camps and access points. Fishing is good on the pond and there is a long fishing pier only a short walk down the Lassiter Trail behind the visitor center. At the boat ramp, small boats with trolling motors can be launched and largemouth bass, crappie, bluegill, and chain pickerel can be caught.

Besides the primitive tent camp areas, there is a family camping area on a side road off Hwy 158 near the park entrance. There are twenty camp-

sites on a loop road for trailer or tent camping. All sites have grills and picnic tables. There aren't electrical hookups, or a dump station, but there is a washhouse with drinking water, restrooms, and showers. A nice trail with a boardwalk wanders from the back of the campground to the fishing pier and to the visitor center. Because the park is near a swamp and lowland, good insect repellent is recommended for campers, hikers, and paddlers.

For hikers and bikers, Merchants Millpond has five trails to explore. The 7-mile Lassiter Trail winds in a long loop from the visitor center through the forests and back. We hiked part of this trail to points on the pond and also hiked some of the scenic Coleman Trail which can be found further down Millpond Road, on the other side of the pond, where there is a parking lot and picnic area. Another trail nearby is the 2.25-miles Bennetts Creek Trail as well as the Bennetts Creek Paddle Trail which follows down the creek toward Gatesville to another backcountry camp area. We saw a number of visitors heading out to canoe the day we visited and also saw anglers trying their luck off the fishing pier.

Lumber River State Park

Coastal Plain Region- Robeson + Counties
Park Address: 2819 Princess Ann Road, Orrum, NC 27027
Park Size: 11,250 acres   Month Visited:June
Directions: To reach Princess Ann Access area of the park, from I-95 south of Lumberton, turn left on Hwy 74 east. Exit on S. Creek Rd (#2225) and follow through Orrum. At the Barnesville Freewill Baptist Church, turn left on Princess Ann Road to park.

Park Description:

Unlike most state parks contained in one area, Lumber River State Park includes 11,259 acres at different locations along a fifty-mile stretch of the Lumber River. The park begins at Chalk Banks Access Point at Wagram, NC, and follows a winding route through mostly remote areas to its end at the Princess Ann Access Point at Orrum, NC. The Lumber River was designated in 1978 as a recreational water trail, in 1981 as a national canoe trail, and in 1989 it became a state park. Along the blackwater of the Lumber River many native American artifacts have been found and the river has many unique ecological factors as well as being a popular recreation corridor for boating, fishing, and other activities out of doors.

The park has three designated sections, from Wagram to Orrum, the (1) scenic; (2) recreational; and (3) natural. The first two sections of the park are more remote and the latter more accessible. The park has 24 primitive campsites along its way, multiple paddle launch access points, and 24 possible float trips. The points at either end, Chalk Banks and Princess Ann, have more camping and picnic facilities and are more developed that the other points.

We chose to visit the Princess Ann end of the park, which contains about 1,054 acres of parkland. It's a scenic stretch on the river with a small visitor center, a nice picnic area and pavilion, good restrooms, a group camp, two primitive campgrounds, and a fine boat ramp for launching small boats, canoes, or kayaks. The park has no canoe or kayak rentals so you will need to bring your own in order to boat. Although remote in location, we were pleased at how lovely the area was. Old cypress trees grew along the river banks and the grounds of the park were very scenic.

At the park, we talked with a camper who often came to camp and fish and to three young men who brought their boats in for a float trip down the river. Fishing is good on the Lumber River and anglers can

fish from boat or river bank, catching largemouth bass, catfish, black crappie, bluegill, chain pickerel, and redbreast sunfish. Paddlers putting in at Princess Ann can paddle up to Pea Ridge, Piney Island, or Buck Landing where they can find primitive campsites and access points. Paddlers may spot otters, muskrats, ducks, and even alligators on the river. Insect repellent is advised for all campers and visitors.

While at Princess Ann, we walked the nice well-maintained trail to the Group Campsite and also explored the trail leading to one of the primitive campsites. We also hiked the 1.5-mile Princess Ann Trail. This trail begins near the picnic shelter to walk into the woods and along the river. The trail rises along a ridge above the river for great views and walks over a 100-foot boardwalk to wind its way to a big observation deck out on the river. The deck looks out over a spot called Griffin's Whirl, a unique area of the river where a reverse stream flow occurs. You will find benches in different spots around the park, nice places to just sit quietly and listen to the birds singing.

Lake Waccamaw State Park

Coastal Plain Region - Columbus County
Park Address: 1866 State Park Drive, Lake Waccamaw, NC 27027
Park Size: 2,398 acres   Month Visited: June
Directions: From I-95, travel southeast on Hwy 74 to Hwy 76. Turn left on Hwy 76, passing through Whiteville. Exit right on Old Lake Rd which becomes Fire Tower Road. Turn left on Sam Potts Hwy 214. Follow to right on Jefferson Road. Travel Jefferson to turn left on Bella Coola Rd. Follow along lake's edge to left on State Park Rd into the park.

Park Description:

Lake Waccamaw State Park lies along the shoreline of Lake Waccamaw, which spreads like a giant oval basin over 9,000 acres and almost 14 square miles. The main section of the park lies on the eastern banks of the lake. Here you will find the visitor center, picnic area, primitive camping area, trails with boardwalks out to the lake, and a popular swim area.

No one really knows how the Carolina bays, or lakes, came to be, but they are unique ecologically. Most are shallow, ranging from eight to twelve feet in depth, and typically are rain fed. They range in size from small bays to large ones and Lake Waccamaw is the largest bay in North Carolina, thought to be 10,000 to 15,000 or more years old. The lakes are called bays because of the

abundance of Sweet, Loblolly, and Red Bay trees that grow around them. Sometimes the waters of bays look a little tea or rust-colored due to the acidity of the water but the waters are often surprisingly clear. It is believed this area of North Carolina was once a shallow sea as a whale fossil was discovered in the lake, which is on display along with other artifacts in the visitor center's small museum.

In the 1700s, the Waccamaw-Sioven Indian tribes lived and hunted around the lake area and later when settlers came the area was heavily logged, especially for cypress trees, and many of the large trees were removed. In 1926 the Waccamaw Dam was built by the state, to try to keep the lake from shrinking, and the state park was established in 1976.

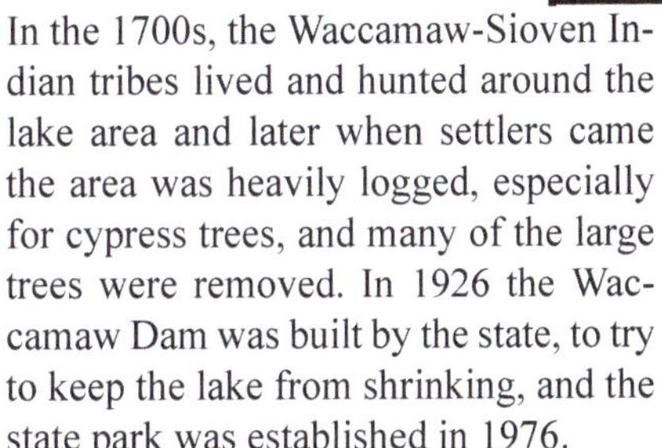

Our exploration of Lake Waccamaw began at the visitor center just inside the park. It's a beautiful building and we enjoyed seeing the exhibits inside, including the whale fossil, and learning about the area and its history. The park has several hiking trails and we took a walk from the visitor center on the longest of the park's trails, the 4-mile Lakeshore Trail. The ranger told us the trail would lead to one of the park's long boardwalks so we could get our first good look at the lake. From the end of the boardwalk the view was stunning across the marsh grasses. After spraying on a little insect repellent, we walked along some of the 0.65-mile Loblolly Trail and on the 1.8 miles Pine Woods Trail, both also starting near the center. Both these trails were thick with pines, bay trees, and oaks. In the right season you can spot carnivorous plants like the Venus Flytrap on these trails.

We were also told wildflowers are pretty here in the spring.

Back in the car, we followed the park road to the picnic and camping area. We found tables and grills there under the trees and discovered nearby the primitive camping area, especially nice for tent camping. The Sand Ridge Nature Trail, an 0.75-mile loop walk, begins near the picnic area and along the way the trees are marked to help identify the route. This trail also leads back to four primitive group camping areas.

Our favorite spot here was the Lake Waccamaw Overlook. A path, and then a long boardwalk, leads out to a shaded pavilion with rest benches and then directly to the lake. This is the park's designated swim area, an especially scenic place, and wide stairs lead down into the water. Because the water is so shallow in Lake Waccamaw, you'll often see visitors standing in the water far from the shore, where usually they would be in deep water over their heads. We talked with several families having fun on the warm June day we visited, all swimming and enjoying the water and the sun. At the end of the long dock are benches on a broad overlook deck where you can sit and look out over the beauty of the wide expanse of Lake Waccamaw. Broad steps from the end of the overlook give more easy access to the water. This is a spot where you wish you could linger and stay longer to enjoy an afternoon in the sunshine.

Fifty-two species of game and non-game fish in Lake Waccamaw make the lake popular for fishing. The park has a scenic boat access near the beginning of the park, good for kayaks, canoes, and small boats but there is a larger boat access, the North Carolina Wildlife Boat Ramp on Canal Cove Road on the other side of the lake. This double boat ramp has a large parking lot, a marina area, docks and piers, making it a beautiful spot. The Wildlife Resource Commission stocks the lake with largemouth bass, bluegill, redbreast sunfish, and shellcracker. There are also three endemic fish, the size of small minnows, like the Waccamaw Silverside, Killifish, and Darter, that can only be found in these waters. The entire area has an interesting ecosystem with many unusual plants and animals.

A drive around the lake is fun to take and winds to the small Waccamaw Dam and a long fishing pier where the Lakeshore Trail ends. Along the way, the road passes along the edge of the town of Lake Waccamaw, where there are stores, historic

spots, and restaurants to explore. Watch for the beautiful Lake Shore Bed and Breakfast inn with a boat ramp across the street from it and for Dale's Seafood restaurant with lovely views over the water to enjoy while you eat. A cute historic spot to also see is the Lake Depot Museum in an old train station, with interesting area artifacts. Enjoy your visit and take lots of photos.

Singletary Lake State Park

Coastal Plain Region- Bladen County
Park Address: 67-7 NC Hwy 53E, Kelly, NC 28448
Park Size: 1,221 acres   Month Visited: June
Directions: From I-95 east of Fayetteville, exit onto Hwy 210/53 east/Cedar Creek Road, staying right on 53 when the road splits. Follow Hwy 53 southeast to park entrance on left.

Park Description:

Singletary State Park is centered around another of North Carolina's shallow, bay lakes. It is one of the larger bays, about 4,000 feet in diameter with 4 miles of shoreline, its depth rarely more than 11 feet. Around the lake are loblolly, sweet bay and red bay trees, along with cedar and cypress—many of the old cypress trees growing right out in the waters. Fish varieties are limited, due to the acidity of the waters, but anglers can enjoy catching yellow perch.

In the 1930s the National Park Service began buying up land around Singletary Lake for recreational purposes and the Civilian Conservation Corps (CCC) then built many of the structures now in the park. In 1939, the government transferred management of the park to North Carolina for a state park. Unlike most state parks Singletary has always been more of a "group camp" park and it is not well-developed for public use. In fact, the park was originally called Singletary Group Camp and was not open to the public to visit until recent years. Now visitors are allowed into the park, from 8-5 when the gates are open, to fish, hike, or put in a small boat at the lake, but checking in at the visitor center—especially when camps are in session—is still encouraged.

There are two group camps at Singletary, Camp Ipacac and Camp Loblolly. Camp Ipacac, named for a medicinal herb, was built by the CCC in 1939, with rustic red buildings. With ten cabins, it can house 92 campers, has a mess hall and restrooms. The newer camp, Camp Loblolly, built in 1984 with gray buildings, will house 48 campers and also has a mess hall and restrooms. Both camps share a basketball court, beach volleyball court, horseshoes, grills, and picnic area. The camps are only open to verifiable organizations of 20 persons or more, Ipacac open April through October, and Loblolly open year-round.

In addition to the visitor center area, the park has an Educational Building that accommodates up to 30 people and can be rented by the public. There is also a small hut available for through hikers on the Mountains to Sea Trail, and the Canebrake Family Cabin is open to the general public for weekly rentals. The cabin has three bedrooms, a kitchen, bath, and an outdoor charcoal grill, and picnic area on a shady site.

A side trail near the Educational Building leads down to a 500-foot-long pier reaching far out into the lake. It is primarily used by the group camps, and swimming from the pier is only permitted for group campers. Canoes are provided for camper use, but visitors can bring their own canoes, kayaks or watercraft (with electric motors) to put into the lake at the inlet toward the back of the park.

There is a nice one-mile easy CCC Loop Trail that that can be accessed from several points around the park, nice for campers and visitors. The more adventurous might talk to the rangers about other trails in the Bay Tree Lake State Natural Area or in the Turkey Oak Natural Area. Rangers sometimes lead hikes into these less developed park sections.

Although Singletary is a pretty park to stop and see, for a more well-developed state park designed for public use, we'd advise visiting Jones Lake State Park, about 30 miles from Singletary, with camping, a public swim beach, boat ramps, picnic areas, and trails.

Jones Lake State Park

Coastal Plain Region- Bladen County
Park Address: 4117 NC Hwy 242N, Elizabethton, NC 28337
Park Size: 2208 acres   Month Visited: June
Directions: From I-95 east of Fayetteville, follow NC Hwy 53 East for appx. 40 miles. Turn left on NC Hwy 242 north for 2 miles to park entrance.

Park Description:

  Adjacent to Bladen Lakes State Forest, Jones Lake State Park is home to two natural Carolina Bay lakes, Jones Lake and Salter Lake. The main developed area of the park is on the southeast side of Jones Lake, a large lake 8,000 feet in diameter. Looking at an aerial view of the park, both lakes look almost like perfect circles.

  Like the other bay lakes we visited, Jones Lake is shallow, seldom deeper than seven to eight feet, even far from shore. The water is highly acidic so not many plants grow in or near the waters, and the acid causes the lake to be tea or rust colored. Few fish can live in the acidity but anglers do catch yellow perch, catfish, pickerel, and some blue-spotted sunfish. Fishing from boat or bank is popular at Jones Lake and there is also a lovely fishing pier reaching far out into the lake. Because of the depth of the lake only canoes, kayaks, and small craft with 10 horsepower motors or less can use the lake, and the park rents canoes and paddleboats in the summer.

We started our exploration of this park at the large visitor center. This is a very attractive facility with a small museum or exhibit hall, telling about how bay lakes were formed and about their ecology. Visitors can enjoy these interesting bay lakes today because the federal government purchased the lakes in the 1930s. The Civilain Conservation Corps (CCC) and Resettlement

Administration programs developed parks around the bay lakes and built recreation buildings, trails, and pavilions for the public to enjoy. In 1939 the federal government turned Jones Lake over to the state and it became the first state park in North Carolina for African Americans, before desegregation.

Behind the Visitors Center is a broad shaded picnic area along the lake. There are fifteen tables and grills here and several pavilions. Two of the pavilions are large ones and the largest, with two fireplaces, can be rented and will accommodate groups up to 300 people. Also along the shore was a beautiful, broad white sand beach. The park has roped off a large section of the lake for swimming, with lifeguards and a concessions stand in summer. Many families were enjoying the lake on the warm June day when we visited. Beside the swim area is

a long pier reaching out into the water, where the rental canoes and paddleboats are kept, and beside the swim area is a boat ramp where small craft can put in. We loved this pretty spot with its views across the water.

Not far from the visitor center on a side road is the park's campground for tent, trailer, and RV camping. There are twenty sites in the family campground loop with restrooms and a bathhouse. Six of the sites have full RV hook-ups for water, sewer, and electric but all the sites are scenic and shaded with grills or fire rings and picnic tables.

Jones Lake has several hiking trails, which have carried different names over time. The longest, the four mile Bay Trail, loops all the way around Jones Lake and is accessible from the campground or from the picnic area. We hiked this trail from the picnic grounds along the lake to an observation point and to the long fishing pier.

On the other side of the picnic area, beyond the boathouse, the 1-mile Cedar Loop Trail travels in an easy hike along the lake side, over a sand ridge, and then through a bay forest. An access point to the Bay Trail can be found at the back of the loop, traveling on around the lake. We'd advise good shoes and insect repellent on all the park trails, and especially on those leading away from the main recreation areas and into less traveled portions of the park, since many walk through some boggy, low areas. Check with

74

rangers because of this, as certain trail sections are not always accessible after a lot of rain.

Salters Lake is managed by the park as a natural area and is not developed. However, you can walk there from the main park on the 1-mile Salters Lake Trail which begins from the back side of Jones Lake branching off the Bay Trail. If you hike both the Bay Trail and Salter Lake Trail, the hike is 5.8 miles, out-and-back, and takes about an hour and forty minutes to walk. All the areas around Salter Lake are more primitive and you should check with the park rangers about visiting this part of the park or any areas of the Bladen Lake State Forest, which adjoins the park. The 32,950-acre forest is the largest state-owned forest in North Carolina and it is a working forest with logging, farming, and other works ongoing, including hunting in season. Also the area has alligators and a large variety of snakes and reptiles.

Jones Lake isn't far from nearby Elizabethton, only four miles away, where park visitors and campers will find a variety of restaurants, shops and stores, a White Water Park, the large Cape Fest ATV park, Brown's Creek Bike Trail, a winery and vineyard.

Cliffs of the Neuse State Park

Coastal Plain Region- Wayne County
Park Address: 240 Entrance Road, Seven Springs, NC 28578
Park Size: 1,097 acres   Month Visited: October
Directions: Travel Hwy 70 into Goldsboro, following 70/13 through town. Beyond Goldsboro at Elroy, take NC Hwy 111 south for about eight miles. Look for the Park Entrance Road on left after crossing the Neuse River.

Park Description:

The Cliffs of the Neuse State Park, which opened in 1945, sits above 90-foot bluffs on the southern banks of the Neuse River. The river was named by an early English explorer Arthur Barlowe in 1584 for the Neusiok Indians. The word Neusiok, or Neuse, means "peace." The entire river is 250 miles in length and many interesting artifacts have been discovered on its shores and in its waters.

We found this a beautiful and interesting park to visit. A long scenic wooded drive led into the park and to the large, new Visitor Center. There we picked up a map, learned about the park's history, and enjoyed the exhibits. Near the center sat a large picnic area with many tables and a big brick pavilion ideal for group gatherings. We soon found more picnic tables on the sprawling patio behind the center, looking out across the park's 11-acre lake. This lovely man-made lake has a broad sandy swim beach, showers and changing area, and a concession stand all spread around scenic grounds. There are swim rafts in the lake and a diving platform. Boat rentals, including canoes, kayaks, paddleboards, and pedal boats, are available for rent at the boathouse. The day we visited, one of the park rangers was giving lessons in paddleboarding, which we enjoyed watching.

The park has seven trails, all easy to moderate to walk. One of the park's seven trails, the 1.9-miles Lake Trail, winds around the back of the lake to cross on a bridge and return to the visitor center. Across the street from the visitor center two other trails begin, the 0.4-mile Longleaf Trail and the 0.4-mile Old Wagon Path. The latter parallels the park road and leads to the cliffs area of the park.

Beyond the visitor center on the left, a side road winds to the park's campground area, tucked around a shady loop. There are thirty-two wooded sites here, for tents or trailers, 12 with water and electric and a bathhouse. The camping area also has three camper cabins, available for rental each with a fire pit, grill, and picnic table. The winding, quiet roads in the campground and throughout the park provide a nice place for bikers, too.

The main park road ends in a loop turnaround beside a large parking area. To the right a path bordered by a rail fence leads along the cliffs above the Neuse River. The 90-foot-high cliffs or bluffs extend

for over 600 yards with different layers of shale, sand, clay, and seashells, creating a diversity of colors in the cliffsides. An observation area reaches out from the path from the trail at its lower end, offering closer views of the cliffs and across and down the river. It is believed the cliffs formed millions of years ago and it is easy to see why a riverboat trip to see them in past eras was a tourist attraction.

Near the observation deck, two of the park's trails begin, the Galax Trail and the Bird Trail, both easy loop trails and each less than a half mile in length. The Bird Trail crosses Still Creek along its path, where whiskey stills were once located. A grist mill that once processed grain used to sit along Mill Creek behind the Galax Trail. On both trails you might see Spanish moss draping off the trees and flowering dogwoods and jasmine in the spring. There is also good fishing along the banks of Still Creek and at many points on the Neuse River where largemouth bass, bluegill, and catfish can be caught.

After returning to the parking area, walk to the left to find the park's museum. The brick building has creative dioramas and audiovisuals that tell about the history of the area and its early inhabitants. A trail near the museum leads to the park's amphitheater in a scenic outdoor setting, where park rangers often give educational talks or programs. Another trail and a side road lead to the park's primitive group camp.

Near the museum and amphitheater is also the beginning of the Spanish Moss Trail. This short 0.5-mile trail leads in a loop down to the Neuse River and back, a good spot for fishing or a fine place to put in or tie up a canoe or kayak. Although rated moderate, the trail has steep steps leading downhill and back uphill again, making the trail a little more challenging for many.

It would be easy to enjoy a nice day at this park, with so many things to do and see. Side trips could be planned to nearby Seven Springs or to Kinston to see the 500-ton hull of the old ironclad Civil War ship the CSS Neuse, built in 1863. It caught fire and sank in the Neuse River but was later excavated and reassembled at the CSS Neuse Civil War Interpretive site.

History Note:

The Cliffs of the Neuse State Park is only 3.8 miles from the old town of Seven Springs, once known as Whitehall after planter William Whitefield. The name of the town changed over time since seven mineral springs, each with a different chemical content, could be found in the town within a short distance of each other. In the late 1800s and early 1900s, several lavish local hotels and resorts were built so visitors could come to "take the waters," known for their healing and curative qualities.

The area became a mecca for society. Visitors to the resorts were also entertained with riverboat rides upstream to see the cliffs of the Neuse. One of the hotels, the old Seven Springs Hotel, stayed in business until after World War II in the 1940s. Still standing, it is a private residence today. The town of Seven Springs has a number of historic sites and buildings, and it holds "Old Timey Days" every spring linked to its past history.

Medoc Mountain State Park

Coastal Plain Region - Halifax County
Park Address: 1540 Medoc State Park Road, Hollister, NC 27844
Park Size: 2,893 acres   Month Visited: October
Directions: From I-95, take exit 160 at NC Hwy 561 and travel west nine miles to the park entrance. Follow the park road, state road 1322, into the park and to the park office.

Park Description:

This is a small pleasant park with tent and trailer camping, picnic spots, and a children's playground. It also offers fishing, paddling, and canoeing on Little Fishing Creek which runs 2.5 miles in the park. Stop at the visitor center after driving into the park and enjoy the exhibits showing plants and animals that can be found in the park. Next to the center look for the 0.5-mile Habitat Adventure Trail, a great family loop-walk with educational signs.

The park's highlights are its hiking, biking, and equestrian trails. One of the trails popular for biking and hiking, the 0.75-mile Bear Swamp Trail, begins right across the road from the park office at a large kiosk. The trail follows through the woods to a bridge over Bear Swamp Creek and on to intersect with several other trails near Spring Branch. Two longer bike trails, the 3.3-mi Saponi and the 5.3-mi Pyrite, intersect for a longer bike ride. Further down the main road is a pullover and trail leading to a Paddle Access spot on Fishing Creek. The shallow creek is perfect for beginning paddlers with slow flowing waters and few obstacles along the way.

A left turn down the road leads into the main section of the park where you'll find the park's campgrounds, a picnic area, playground, and access to more park trails. Off the campsite road is a group camp area and a scenic figure-eight road winding into the main family campground. The campground has 34 sites tucked around the shady road, 12 with electric hookups, a nice bathhouse, and a sanitary dump. Within walking distance from the campground are access points to the creek for fishing for bass, bluegill, chain pickerel, or redbreast sunfish.

Either a short walk, bike ride, or drive from the campground area leads to a large scenic park with a big playing field for games, a large pavilion and picnic tables, and a wonderful playground for children with a nice diversity of play equipment. Several trails branch out from the playground area, the 1.0-mile easy Campground Loop, the 1.75-mile Bluff Loop Trail, and the 0.75-mile Stream Loop Trail, leading to Fishing Creek and back. Additionally, the 1.25-mile Discovery Loop Trail winds north along the creek to cross a bridge and connect to the Summit Loop Trail, 3-miles in length but over four miles total, if you add the walk to get to the trailhead and back.

Despite the name of the park, there is no mountain at Medoc. The term "Medoc," coined from a province in France famous for vineyards, came from the vineyards once in the area and the term "Mountain" from an ancient range of mountains that used to rise high in this region. Now all that remains of these mountains is a hill 325-feet in elevation. As you hike around the Summit Loop Trail, you will never see any obvious summits or find any mountain views, but you will enjoy a scenic woods trail circling a peaceful hillside and you might spot a small family cemetery and remnants of an old Boy Scout camp along the way.

Beyond the campground section a road leads to another small picnic area and shelter with access to an equestrian camp and a multitude of bridle trails. There is also a second paddle and canoe access point under the bridge over the creek. Although small, this park is a peaceful gem, scenic, well-maintained and offering good star-gazing at night.

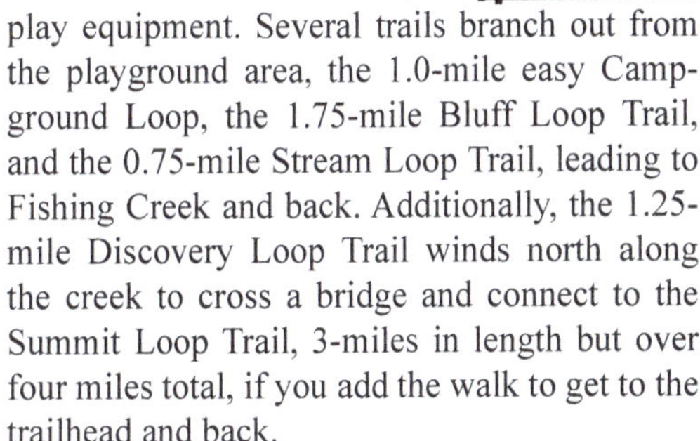

Carvers Creek State Park

Coastal Plain Region - Cumberland County
Park Address: 2505 Long Valley Road, Spring Lake, NC 28390
Park Size: 4,530 acres   Month Visited: October
Directions: From Hwy 24, in Spring Lake, nine miles north of Fayetteville, turn right on Manchester Road and follow to Long Valley Road. Turn left on Long Valley Road and follow into park and park office on right.

Park Description:

Carvers Creek, one of North Carolina's newest parks, was established in 2005 as the 42nd state park and opened its doors in 2013. Located in the Sandhills area not far from Fayetteville and Fort Bragg, the new park is still in development stages, offering hiking, biking, picnicking, fishing and a wonderful opportunity to enjoy a diverse slice of nature. The park has two sections separated by a 15-minute drive. The main section is at Long Valley Road where the park office is located. The second, the Sandhills Access, begins at a parking area on McCloskey Road, and consists of only hiking, biking, and horseback trails, all popular with locals.

Plan to go first to the main park section to see the Long Valley Farm, which was James Stillman Rockefeller's winter home. A dirt road winds from the park office to the historic 1,240-acre farm, built by Rockefeller and donated to the public after his death. At this time the only route to the farm property is by walking the 2-mile (4 mi RT) dirt road, called The Rockefeller Loop Trail, so come prepared with good walking shoes, bug spray, and water before you set out to explore. Along the sandy road you will enjoy looking up at the tall longleaf pines and stopping to read the interpretive signs, that tell about the grasslands and ecology of the area.

You can't miss the Long Valley Farm sign as you near the end of the road. Behind it you'll see the Rockefeller's big, white two-storied house, built in 1938 and now on the National Register of Historic Places. Also on the property are a number of different outbuildings, several historically significant, and a 100-acre lake called McDairmid Millpond. The old house and property are beautiful and the park gives tours of the house about once a month. As you walk around the property, watch for the old spring house built over an artesian well, a small amphitheater, and a huge mag-

nolia tree behind the house, its branches almost touching the ground.

On the lake is a big pavilion and observation deck where the Rockefellers entertained many dignitaries, and you will also spot a canoe house near the front of the lake. From this point, park rangers sometimes give canoe-tours into the cypress marshes at the back of the lake. Following around the side of the lake is the 0.75-mile Cypress Point Loop Trail, leading back to the cypress marsh section of the lake and veering off to many nice fishing and picnic spots along the way.

Back at the park office, you can get information about and directions to the Sandhills section of the park and drive over to hike some of its many trails, lacing through a pine forest. A good trail to first explore is the main Longleaf Pine Trail, 4 miles in length and beginning at the parking area. All the other Sandhills trails branch off of this trail.

Carvers Creek's master plan is to buy lands between the Long Valley Farm and the Sandhills Access section to connect the two areas and in time to add camping facilities, and a full range of other recreational amenities. The park also plans to soon convert the Rockefeller Home into an enlarged park office with interpretive exhibits, meeting rooms, and other community activities. The park, even now in its early stages, is interesting to visit and we enjoyed seeing the old Rockefeller home and stepping back into the past to learn about the park's early origins.

Raven Rock State Park

Coastal Plain Region - Harnett County
Park Address: 3009 Raven Rock Road, Lillington, NC 27546
Park Size: 4,810 acres   Month Visited: October
Directions: From I-40 at Greensboro, take Hwy 421 south through Sanford toward Lillington. Past the small town of Mamers, turn left on Hwy 1314, Raven Rock Road, and follow into park.

Park Description:

Raven Rock Park is named for the ravens that used to roost on the ledges of the 150-foot-high rock cliffs that stretch for more than a mile along the Cape Fear River. The cliffs were gradually sculpted and carved out by water and erosion over millions of years, and the park, known predominately for its beautiful hiking trails, is highly visited.

A long road winds into the park to arrive at the main visitor center. The fine facility with outdoor picnic tables to one side has an interpretative exhibit hall, a Native American Indian display, classrooms, an amphitheater, and spacious entry where you can pick up brochures, maps, and souvenirs. Behind the center is a big picnic shelter and the beginning of the 0.3-mile interpretive Longleaf Loop Trail that winds into the woods behind the center.

The park has 26 miles of hiking trails, 13.5 miles of bike trails, plus 8 miles of equestrian trails across the river on the River Road. With a short time to visit the park, we couldn't hike all the trails, but we explored the most popular ones. The most hiked trail is the 2.1-mile Raven Rock Loop Trail that leads to Raven Rock cliffs and to an overlook across the Cape Fear River. The trail begins on a broad, flat trail not far behind the visitor center. The walk is easy at first, with small bridges over creeks, and other trails branching off along the way. At about a mile, a spur of the trail veers right, continuing to a set of 136 winding stairs that climb down to the river below the cliffs. A short path there wanders along the bank, offering stunning views of the cliffs and overhangs. For those not in good physical shape, the steep stairs down and back can be a challenge, even with benches along the way for an occasional rest. Back at the trail intersection again, continuing left leads in about a half mile to an overlook with a rock wall around it and rest benches beside it. From the overlook are vistas across the Cape Fear River winding far

below, a reminder of how high the park sits above the river valley.

Another nice hike to walk is the the 0.6-mile Fish Traps Trail to the Cape Fear River's edge where big flat rocks sit in the water with rapids and cascades tumbling around them. Here, too, steep steps climb down to the river and back. For a longer hike, add the Northington Ferry Trail, traveling about a mile down to remnants of the Northington lock and dam on the river. A more moderate hike is to walk part, or all, of the 5-mile Campbell Loop Trail. It begins at the parking lot near the visitor center and heads east, crossing a wide bridge over Campbell Creek along the way before heading on to the river. At appx 2.5 miles is a side trail to one of the park's wilderness camps and, a short distance later, Lanier Falls Trail branches off, leading to Lanier rapids on the river, a pretty spot.

To enjoy more time at Raven Rock State Park and to hike more of its trails, you can now camp in the park's new campground off Moccasin Branch Road just outside the park entrance. This campground includes 9 RV sites, 15 tent sites, a bathhouse, and 6 cute rental cabins on a nice loop road not far from the Mountain Laurel bicycle loop trail. There is also a primitive canoe camp, about 2.2 miles from the visitor center, on the Cape Fear River with paddle access at the end of the Little Creek Loop Trail. Get out your hiking boots and come and enjoy this memorable and beautiful park.

Weymouth Woods State Park
and Sandhills Nature Preserve

Coastal Plain Region - Moore County
Park Address: 1024 N Bragg Rd, Southern Pines, NC 28387
Park Size: 915 acres   Month Visited: October
Directions: North of Fayetteville and Fort Bragg, take Hwy 690 east to Vass, then turn south on Hwy 1 to Southern Pines. Turn left on Saunders Blvd and follow to its end, turning left on Bethseda Road, staying right into Fort Bragg Road to park entrance on left.

Park Description:

This park lies right on the boundary of the coastal plain in the Sandhills Region of the state and is only 35 miles from Fayetteville. The main part of the park, the Weymouth Estate, was donated to the park by the Boyd family in 1963. Two more nearby sections, the Boyd and the Paint Hill Tract have been since added, all to help preserve this unique nature preserve. The park's main focus are the stands of tall longleaf pines throughout the park, many 250 to 400 years old.

Begin your exploration of this park at the main Weymouth Woods Tract on Fort Bragg Road. A fine visitor center there has exhibits and information about the park. Next to the visitor center is the Sandhills Discovery Room with interesting exhibits, learning activities, and a Pinelands Puppet Pavilion for children's educational shows. The park rangers give talks and conduct hikes at the park at scheduled times for visitors and school groups. Behind the Discovery Room is a small garden, the Mac Goodwin Memorial Wildlife Garden, a few picnic tables, and a rest bench looking out over the pine forest.

Do plan to take one or two of the well-maintained trails while visiting. The park has about 7-8 miles of hiking trails, all easy trails for most all ages and abilities to walk. Two that are readily accessible from the visitor center and parking area are the 0.3-mile Bowers Bog Trail and the 1.0-mile Pine Barrens Trail. The short Bower's Bog Trail begins across from the center and loops through the woods and back. The trail, only taking about

10 minutes to walk, gives a good look at the tall longleaf pines in the park preserve. Be sure to watch for huge pine cones along the way, a reminder of the size of the trees in the park.

The Pine Barrens Trail begins behind the visitor center and makes a one-mile loop around the forest. For a longer 4-5-mile walk take the Gum Swamp Trail to the bridge over James Creek and into the short 0.1-mile Moccasin Crossing Trail. At its end turn right on Holly Road Trail and follow to the Pine Island Trail. This loop path leads through swampland and over a long board-walk, showing you more of the park's diversity. You can return the way you came or follow Lighter Stump Trail back to the center. Do carry a park hiking map with you as the trails throughout the park cross and intersect at many points.

The park office can give you directions to the two other park sections if you want to explore more trails. At the Boyd Tract on Connecticut Avenue a 1-mile trail, called Round Timer Trail, leads to the oldest known living longleaf pine in the world and past several other incredibly tall and ancient trees preserved in the park. In the spring all sections of the park come alive with shows of wildflowers and the park is home to nearly five hundred species of plants and an abundance of wildlife. If you have time, take a picnic to nearby Reservoir Park or go to see the Weymouth Center for the Arts and Humanities, next to the Boyd Tract of the park, and to the historic Boyd House and gardens. The Boyd House is listed in the National Register of Historic Places and was awarded a certificate of achievement by the National Wildlife Federation.

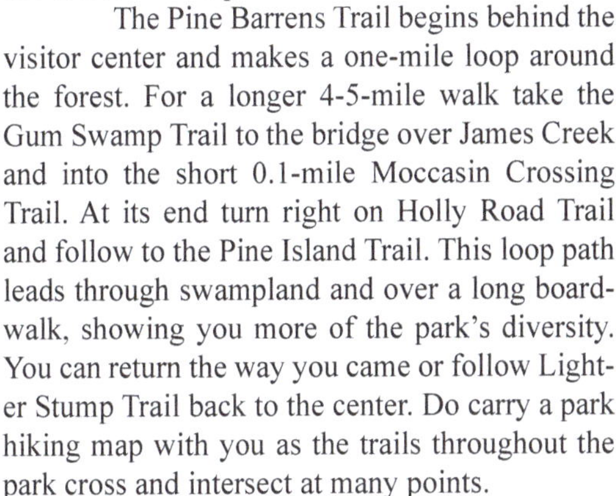

Morrow Mountain

PIEDMONT REGION STATE PARK INDEX

Kerr Lake State Park 90
William B. Umstead State Park 94
Falls Lake State Park 98
Eno River State Park 102
Occoneechee Mountain State Park 104
Jordan Lake State Park 106
Guilford Courthouse National Military Park 110
Haw River State Park 112
Mayo River State Park 114
Morrow Mountain State Park 116
Hanging Rock State Park 120
Lake Norman State Park 124
Crowders Mountain State Park 128

Piedmont Region
North Carolina
PARKS

Hanging Rock

William B. Umstead

Kerr Lake

Jordan Lake

Kerr Lake State Park Recreation Area

Piedmont Region - Vance & Warren Counties
Park Address: 6275 Satterwhite Point Rd, Hendersonville, NC 27537
Park Size: 3,376 acres   Month Visited: October
Directions: From I-85 above Henderson, NC, take Exit 217, traveling north on Hwy 1319 or Satterwhite Point Road. Follow Satterwhite Point Road about 5-6 miles directly into park and watch for right turn into the Park Office.

Park Description:

The entire Kerr Lake Recreation Area, established in 1981, includes 3,376 acres in different places along the shorelines of the 50,000-acre manmade Kerr Lake. The lake, park, and the John H. Kerr Dam over the border in Virginia were named after North Carolina congressman John H. Kerr who was instrumental in obtaining funding and approval for the project.

As a whole, Kerr Lake State Park has eight access areas around the shoreline of North Carolina in seven main park sections. All seven park sections have fine lake access, at least one boat launch ramp, camping, picnic areas, pavilions, and an assortment of other amenities. The areas are: (1) Satterwhite Point and the J.C. Cooper Campground, (2) Nutbush Bridge, (3) Bullocksville Recreation Area, (4) Hibernia, (5) County Line Recreation Area, (6) Henderson Point, and (7) Kimball Point. All the park areas are popular and can be enjoyed year long.

From Memorial Day to Labor Day and on the weekends in April, May, and September, the park charges entrance fees per vehicle daily. The rest of the year entrance to the park is free.

We started our visit to this park in the main Satterwhite Point area on the southern part of Kerr Lake where the visitor center and park office is located. The large visitor center is a great place to begin. There you will find information, area maps, and individual maps to each section of the park. Since the park's areas are scattered all around the shoreline of Kerr Lake, these maps and brochures are very helpful in finding your way around the park.

Due to time constraints, we only visited the two southernmost areas of the park at Satterwhite Point and at Nutbush Bridge, closer to Hwy 39 and I-85.

Truly, this lake is a stunning, beautiful one, which I'm sure you can see from the photos. I could happily spend a day or two here sitting along the shore enjoying the view, skimming around the lake in a boat, stopping to picnic at one of the picnic tables or nice pavilions. As we drove from the park office toward the peninsula point, we explored every branch-off road along the way. One led down to the Satterwhite Point Marina, a great place to keep a boat or launch one, and a good place to put in canoes or kayaks, too. Near the marina was also a fuel dock and store. The marina, store, and repair shop are

privately owned but exceptionally nice and the owners even have rental cabins on the lake.

Veering back to the main road again led us to a cross road leading over to Shoreline Lane on the other side of the Satterwhite peninsula. Backtracking south brought us to the big J.C. Cooper Campground with 98 campsites. This is a large campground with tent, trailer, and RV camping spaces. It has electric hookup for some sites, water, and a dump station. All sites are shady, a short walk to the lake or lakefront, and there is a boat ramp, a kids' playground, and a hiking trail called the Big Poplar Hiking Trail. The loop road streets are a great place to walk or bike, too.

Leaving the campground and heading north on Shoreline Road again leads to more beautiful spots on the lake to enjoy, culminating at the end of the peninsula at a parking lot with stunning views out across the lake. Nearby are picnic tables, two large pavilions, and a nice community building.

The next loop road on Shoreline Road leads to a defined swim beach area, with a long sandy beach and an inviting roped off swim area. Near the beach are picnic tables, benches in the shade, and a long green lawn for outdoor chairs, blankets, and play for children. As an extra perk, not far down Satterwhite Point Road as you leave this park section is the Kerr County Country Club with a beautiful golf course open to the public.

We also took Nutbush Road and crossed Kerr Lake on a long bridge to explore the Nutbush Bridge park section, set on another scenic peninsula on the lake. Here we found two more campground areas, more pavilions and spots to picnic, two more boat launches, and an event area. Not far from one of the pavilions, near the end of the peninsula, was an outdoor chapel, called the C. H. Guerrant

Memorial Chapel, a lovely place for small services or outdoor weddings.

There are 109 campsites in the two campground areas at Nutbush on shady loop roads near or on the lake. The sites will accommodate a variety of camping trailers and RVs as well as tents. All sites have grills and picnic tables and both camping areas have bathhouses, electric and water hookups, and a sanitary dump. At Nutbush, as at Satterwhite, we found breathtaking views of Kerr Lake and idyllic spots by the water to spend a peaceful day outdoors.

From talking to rangers and other travelers and campers, they all said each of the other sections of the park are equally beautiful with good access to the lake and fine amenities. This entire park is a paradise for those who love to boat, play, and fish on the water. Kerr Lake is one of the best fishing lakes in the United States and many tournaments are held here. Anglers can catch largemouth and striped bass, crappie, and white perch and can fish from the bank, fishing piers or from their boats. Birds and wildlife are abundant in the park and you might hear frogs croaking or an owl hooting at night if you camp. This is a park you shouldn't miss visiting if you are in the Piedmont area of the state.

William B. Umstead State Park

Piedmont Region - Wake County
Park Address: 8801 Glenwood Ave, Raleigh, NC 27617
Park Size: 5,579 acres   Month Visited: October
Directions: Coming east from Greensboro, follow I-40 through southern Durham and into Raleigh. Turn north on I-540/Northern Wake Expressway and then right on Hwy 70/New Raleigh Hwy. Watch for turn to park entrance on right.

Park Description:

This is a city park oasis not far from the heart of downtown Raleigh. It seemed amazing to wind back suddenly into this green and peaceful park after driving through extensive traffic, congested roads, and heavy commercial areas. As you can imagine, it is very popular for the locals and the park is nearly always busy, even during the week. The early park was built in part by the Civilian Conservation Corps and the Works Progress Administration and opened its doors in 1934. It is named for North Carolina's 63rd governor, also an attorney and congressman, in recognition for his many conservation efforts.

We stopped at the main Visitor Center first to pick up brochures and maps and to learn more about the park's history at the exhibit hall. The William B. Umstead Park is rich with amenities. It has three manmade lakes, fishing, kayaking and canoeing, a boat launch, picnic grounds and shelters, a big family campground and group camps, and miles and miles of trails for hiking, biking, and horseback riding. The main and largest section of the park, called the Crabtree Creek area, off Hwy 70, is extensive in itself, but there is also a second park area at Reedy Creek off I-40. In earlier times, the Reedy Creek area was an African American Park until the two parks united in 1966. The two sections connect by a latticework of wilderness trails

but there is no road directly through the park between them, and the drive from one part to the other takes about 15-20 minutes.

One of the park's trails, The Sal's Branch Trail, has a spur link at the visitor center. It is one of the park's 34.5 miles of hiking trails and there are also 13 miles of bike trails and 13 miles of equestrian trails, many of the trails multi-use. The Sal's Branch Trail (2.8-mi) connects to the park's main campground. Twenty-eight tent and trailer campsites sit around the campground's shady loop road, suitable for small camping trailers and tent camping. There is a nice bathhouse but no electrical hookups or facilities for large RVs. The park has three group camp areas, Camp Lapihio and Camp Crabtree in the main park area and Camp Whispering Pines at Reedy Creek. Also, there is a Youth Camp on Sycamore Road across from the Maple Hill Lodge. The old lodge is a historic landmark built in the 1930s with outdoor facilities and fireplaces. With reservations, groups or

individuals can bring sleeping bags for a rustic overnight here.

Continuing down the main road from the visitor center to its end leads to two parking lots. At the first is a picnic area and access to two trails, the easy 0.6-mi Oak Rock Trail, that loops through the woods and back, and an access point to the 2.6-mile Potts Branch Trail that runs to a pretty creek and an old abandoned rock dam. At the second parking lot is another picnic area and pavilion and access to more trails. We took the trail down to Big Lake here, a nice easy walk through the woods and we then followed the end of the Sal's Branch Trail along the lake's banks. There is a boathouse here, with boat rentals in summer, and you'll find rest benches along the way and some rocks to sit down on to take a quiet moment to look across this pretty 55-acre lake. As you'll quickly see, the trails weave and overlap in many areas, so be sure to pick up a map showing the trails and keep it with you so you won't get lost as you hike.

Returning up the main road after exploring the area around Big Lake, we turned down Sycamore Road by Maple Hill Lodge and the Youth Camp to drive to the end of this side road and to another parking area. A fun and easy one mile trail to the left of the parking area leads to the Log Art sculpture, chiseled into a massive oak by two chainsaw artists from the Smoky Mountains named Jerry Reid and Randi Boni. The old tree, a massive red oak, 25 feet in circumference, fell to the ground in 2015. Rather than chopping up the tree, the two chainsaw artists came and spent a week chiseling an assortment of mountain art forms into the tree's trunk, including foxes, bears, a bunny, birds, hoot owls, a squirrel and more. It's a short hike to the old tree, called "Hidden Treasures," and worth the walk to see this unique sculpture.

The trail on the other side of the parking lot leads through a camp area,

including cabins and an old lodge, to wind gradually downhill to Sycamore Lake. We loved this trail and the quiet lake we found at its end. The 25-acre lake is a good spot for fishing from the bank or at the pier found halfway around the lake. The park allows fishing in all three of its lakes and in the connecting streams. Anglers catch crappie, bass, and bluegill from the banks or piers. At Sycamore Lake, we took a rest break in Adirondack chairs built on platforms by the lakeside.

To hike more trails, the park map will show you other trails easily accessed from the Crabtree Creek area of the park or you can drive around to the Reedy Creek Access area to park and find more. There are picnic tables and two pavilions at the Reedy Creek Entrance. A pleasant, easy trail to hike from the parking area is the trail to Reedy Lake, which winds from the road on an open dirt and gravel roadway directly to the 25-acre lake. The lake sits in a pretty spot and it has a fishing pier you can walk out on to enjoy more of the view. This side of the park is especially popular with bikers and horseback riders and with hikers who want a long hike into less visited areas of the park.

The Raleigh-Durham area is blessed that a park was established here in the early 1900s and that the land was bought and preserved. Throughout the U.S., we owe so much to early administrations in our country who bought vast acreages of lands and created parks in them that we still enjoy today.

Falls Lake State Park Recreation Area

Piedmont Region - Durham & Wake County
Park Address: 13394 Creedmoor Road, Wake Forest, NC 27587
Park Size: 5,035 acres   Month Visited: October
Directions: From Hwy 1 at Wake Forest take Hwy 98 west, through Stony Hill, and then turn right on Hwy 50/Creedmoor Road. Follow Creedmoor into park and turn right before crossing the bridge, to stop at the Park Office and Information Center.

Park Description:

    Falls Lake State Park sprawls along the fingers and shores of Falls Lake, which covers 12,410 acres. The park offers boating, camping, swimming, fishing, biking, hiking, picnicking, and a variety of other pleasurable amenities. The lake was created when the Army Corps of Engineers completed the building of Falls Lake Dam on the Neuse River in 1981. The park is less than a thirty-minute drive from Wake Forest, Raleigh, and Durham, and stays busy all year, especially in the summer. Entrance fees are charged from Memorial Day to Labor Day and on weekends in April, May, and September.

    If you have never visited the park before, stop first at the large park office on a side road right before Hwy 50 crosses Stringer Bridge. The center, sitting on a scenic peninsula in the lake, has a nice exhibit area, meeting rooms, and fine lake views behind it. You can get information about the park and its ame-

nities as a whole here and pick up individual brochures on any of the park's seven access areas: (1) Highway 50; (2) Beaverdam Lake; (3) Sandling Beach; (4) Shinleaf Campground; (5) Holly Point Campground; (6) B. W. Wells Ground Campground, and (7) Rolling View Campground and Day-Use Area. All the sections we visited were beautiful and inviting, each with its own unique charm. Be sure to check

with the park office as to what type of boats are allowed in each of the park's access areas, whether gas-powered and electric motorized boats, electric only, or simply non-motorized canoes and kayaks.

The Highway 50 Day-Use area is the closest to the park office and just across the Stringer Bridge to the right off the Creedmoor Road. Easy to access, it has a big parking area at a 6-lane boat launch for all types of motorized and non-motorized boats. This is a great place to boat, ski, fish or swim and enjoy the day. Several picnic areas sit along the water, and walking trails wind between the picnic areas and to the boat launch. At one of the picnic areas is a small loop trail, beginning at the parking area. A side branch

of the trail crosses the small dam over the lake—a nice spot for fishing or for a walk to see some scenic lake views.

Beaverdam Day-Use Area, a short distance up the road, is a bigger access area spreading over several fingers of the lake. A quieter spot, allowing only

electric powered boats, it offers several mountain bike trails and hiking trails, picnic areas, fishing, and swimming. A biking trails map, available through the park office, shows all the trails and provides biker rules. Taking the turn to the left after the entrance fee office leads to a loop road along the lake with a multitude of picnic tables, pavilions, a swim beach, a nice children's playground, swim areas, and a pretty fishing pier. Off this road are two short hiking trails that are a pleasure to walk. The 1.2-mile Duck Cove Trail starts near the lake and the 1.5-mile Fox Trot Trail loops through the woods from a point further along the road. Following the second park road past the entrance station brings visitors to more picnic areas and pavilions with stunning views across the lake, a second long fishing pier, and the start of the mountain bike trailhead.

The Sandling Beach Day Use Area lies to the left side of the road beyond Beaverdam. A beautiful walkway leads down to a a long broad sand beach on the lake. Perfect for small children, the lake is calm here, well-roped off, and visitors can pick up swim vests for their children if they forgot them. A bathhouse with outdoor showers sits nearby, with picnic tables under pretty shade trees, a playground and access to a long trail along the lake, nice for all ages. Off the Sandling Beach road are more picnic sites and pavilions and a scenic 0.7-mile Woodland Nature Trail with interpretive signs, beginning at Shelter #2.

Returning back on Creedmoor Road to Highway 98 again, leads west to the entrances to the Shinleaf Campground and Holly Point Campground areas. Shinleaf is the smaller and quieter campground of the two, only offering tent camping and group camping. Only non-motorized boats, like canoes and kayaks, are allowed at Shinleaf and there are several good trails in the area, including a crossing of the Mountains-to-Sea Trail. Holly Point is a far bigger campground

offering tent, trailer, and RV camping, bathhouses, a dump station, amphitheater, playground, swim beach, and boat dock for all types of boats, and a hiking trail winding through the property. The Small B.W. Wells area nearby is known mainly for its groups camps and trails, for canoeing and kayaking, like to Zeagles Rock, and for the historic B.W. Wells Rockcliff Farm nearby, available for guided tours and hikes.

The last park section we visited, and possibly our favorite, was the Rolling View Campground and Day-Use Area further east off Hwy 98. Almost like a state park in itself, Rolling View has a beautiful campground on three loop trails, with tent, trailer, and RV camping, bathhouses, playground, a big fishing pier, lake access and a dump station. Winding inland leads

to side roads to lovely picnic areas, swim areas, fishing piers, hiking trails, and scenic spots along the lake. On the end of the peninsula at the road's end is a full marina and boat dock, and more picnic spots and wonderful picturesque views across the water—the perfect way to end our visit to the park.

Eno River State Park

Piedmont Region - Durham & Orange County
Park Address: 6101 Cole Mill Road, Durham, NC 27705
Park Size: 4,319 acres   Month Visited: October
Directions: From Interstate 85 heading east toward Durham, exit north on Pleasant Green Road. Follow to left on Cole Mill Road into main part of park and office.

Park Description:

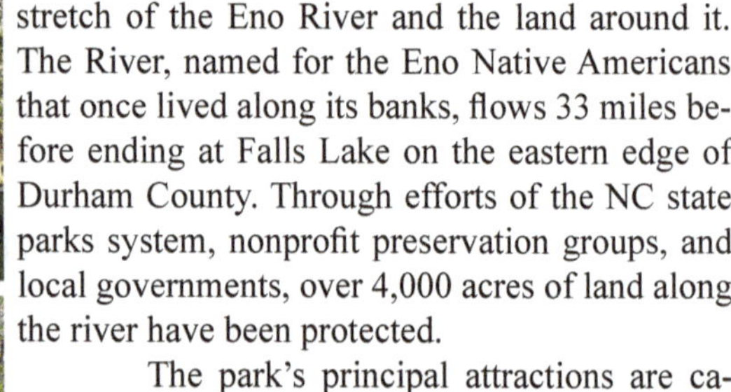

Eno River was established to protect a stretch of the Eno River and the land around it. The River, named for the Eno Native Americans that once lived along its banks, flows 33 miles before ending at Falls Lake on the eastern edge of Durham County. Through efforts of the NC state parks system, nonprofit preservation groups, and local governments, over 4,000 acres of land along the river have been protected.

The park's principal attractions are canoeing, kayaking, and rafting on the scenic Eno River with its Class II Rapids, fishing along the river's banks, hiking on the abundance of park trails, picnicking, and simply enjoying the natural beauty of the area. Camping in the park is only in back country sites and requires a permit.

The park has five major access areas to the river. Most of the park's facilities are concentrated near the park office in the Fews Ford area. After turning left on Cole Mill Road, follow it to the park office, connected to the historic Piper-Cox log cabin. Be sure to get a park map there showing the park roads and trails as many interconnect. The other park areas, Pleasant Green, Cabe Lands, Pump Station, and Cole Mill are mainly access points to the river with parking for boating, fishing, and hiking. Be watchful about paddling or boating when the water is high as the rapids can be dangerous.

We started our exploration by following from the park office to walk down to the river on the 1.5-mile Buckwater Creek Trail. The stair-trail leads down to the Fews Ford crossing at the river, once traveled by early settlers and Indians. Turning right at the crossing leads along the river banks to a section of rocks and rapids, a scenic spot. Several other trails branch in different directions in this area, but we headed across the road next to walk Fanny's Ford Trail and to check out one of the tent camping areas. This trail and campground were named for a Black midwife, Fanny Breeze, who once lived in this area. The trails were rich with fall color

and in the spring there are many wildflowers here.

Driving down the park road in the other direction led past a community building and a shady picnic area and pavilion and the beginning of the Cox Mountain Trail. This is a 4.6-mi trail, but a shorter hike takes you down river and to a long suspension bridge crossing it. This is a pretty spot and on the other side of the river is a group camp area with tent pads and an old log shelter.

Leaving Few Fords, we drove to check out the Cole Mill area. Near the bridge that crosses the river is another picnic area and pavilion, a paddle access point, and several more trails to explore. The approximately 1.8-mile Dunnagan Trail leads along the river. At one point, looking across the river, you can spot the ruins of the old Pump Station that used to supply Durham's water. On the loop walk back watch for the ruins of the old Dunnagan home and look for the small graveyard with Catherine Dunnagan's tombstone and several other unmarked graves. From the parking area, the Cole Mill Trail winds along the river to take you to Bobbits Hole, a favorite swimming hole and fishing spot.

A final interesting trail to walk is the 2-2-mi Cabes Land and Eno Quarry Trail, starting on Howe Road. This loop trail leads to an old quarry near a bend in the river. Throughout the park are many historic sites like these, fun to search out and learn about. Although a small park, Eno River is a beautiful and scenic one with a fine river environment to enjoy.

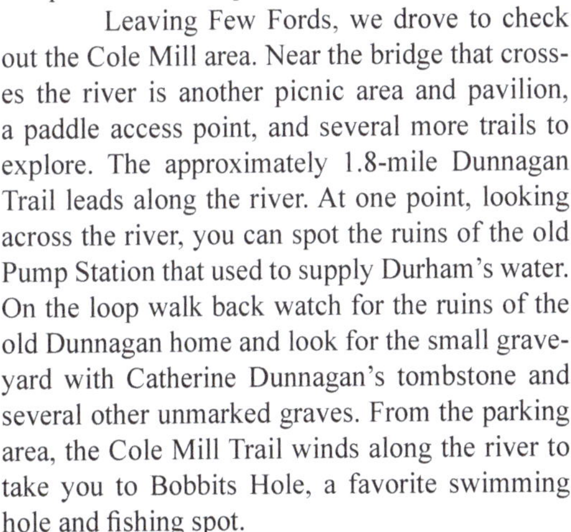

Occoneechee Mtn State Park Natural Area

Piedmont Region - Orange County
Park Address: 635 Virginia Cates Road, Hillsboro, NC 27278
Park Size: 190 acres   Month Visited: October
Directions: From Interstate 85 take exit 164 and follow north on Churton Road. Turn left/east on Mayo at light, left on Orange Grove Road at the stop sign and then right on Virginia Cates Road leading directly into the park.

Park Description:

This small park on the outskirts of Hillsboro, and not far from Durham, is best known for the Occoneechee Mountain at its center, rising 350 feet above the Eno River that flows along the north boundary of the park. A protected natural area, Occoneechee offers scenic beauty and a diversity of wildlife and plants, miles of hiking trails, fishing at two ponds and along the Eno River, and picnicking at tables by the parking area.

The park's name comes from the Occaneechi Indian tribe who once lived in a vlllage on a bend of the Eno. At this time, there is no park office on site and Occoneechee is managed by the Eno River State Park 10 miles away in Durham.

Driving into this pretty park along the entry road, we enjoyed the quiet and the beauty of the fall color and soon spotted the park's two ponds to the right of the road. We pulled into a parking area to get out and walk along the trail by the larger pond, where we saw a few people fishing on the banks. Bass and bream can be caught in the ponds and bluegill, redbreast, bass, and sunfish at spots along the Eno River.

The main parking area is small and picnic tables were scattered on a hillside behind it. We enjoyed watching a young woman practicing yoga moves on one of the tables, savoring the quiet of the area in her own way and she let us snap her photo. Following the continuing gravel roadbed by foot leads to the park's hiking trails and to the ranger's residence. As you walk up this road, watch for a pick-up box beside the trail where you can get a park map. You will need this to help you find your way, since the park trails cross and intersect at several points.

The most popular and longest trail is the 2.2-mile Occoneechee Mountain Loop Trail that winds in a loop around the high bluffs that make up the park, following along the Eno River on its way. Don't miss the short 0.15-mile trail to the summit Overlook beyond the turn to the Brown Elfin Knob Trail

where you can enjoy views out across Hillsborough and over the Eno River Valley. Watch also for a side trail along the river leading about 100 feet to an impressive view of the rock quarry from below. A little further down the trail take the short spur trail to Panther's Den which winds you to another view of rocky bluffs.

A shorter trail to the overlook is the 0.9-mile Chestnut Oak Trail. It cuts more directly through the middle of the park, leading you to the Overlook Trail more quickly. At the summit you wind through some rocky bluffs to come out on a trail along the side of the mountain with a fence along it. There is also a nice bench where you can sit down for a rest or just enjoy the view out over the valley. Another trail, the short Brown Elfin Knob Trail links the Chestnut Oak and Occoneechee Mountain Loop Trail. Note that a private trail near the overlook, not open to the public, leads to a communications tower belonging to Orange County. Despite its small size, this park is very popular with locals, as well as tourists, and is often very busy on the weekends, with access limited if the parking area is full.

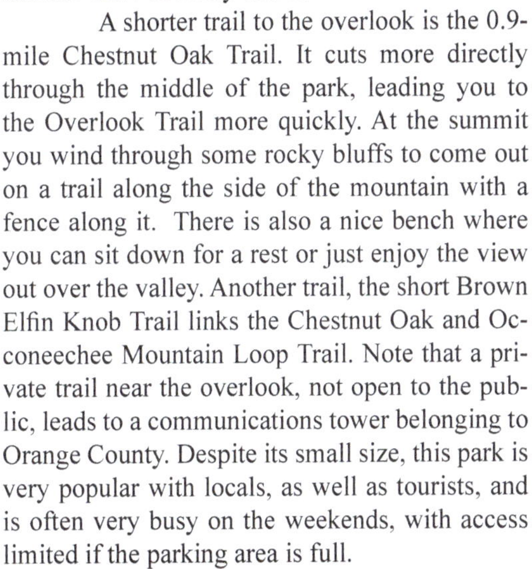

Jordan Lake State Park Recreation Area

Piedmont Region - Chatham County
Park Address: 280 State Park Road, Apex, NC 27523
Park Size: 4,558 acres   Month Visited: October
Directions: From I-40, take NC Hwy 751 south and follow to Hwy 64. Turn right and travel west on 64. Cross Beavercreek Road and continue on Hwy 64 into park to left before the bridge on State Park Road and the Jordan Lake Recreation Visitor Center.

Park Description:

    Authorized by the U.S. Congress, the B. Everett Jordan Lake Dam was completed and the lake filled in 1981, to provide flood control, a good water supply, and to promote conservation and recreation. Jordan Lake Recreation Area, in the state park system, opened in 1982. The park's multiple recreational areas lie along the coves, fingerlike inlets, and open water of the almost 14,000-acre Jordan Lake. A beautiful park, it offers boating, paddling, fishing, picnicking, swimming, camping, hiking, and a multitude of other outdoor activities.

    A large visitor center sits by the lake on a side road just before the Hwy 64 bridge crossing. Visitors can check out the center's fine exhibit room, auditorium and classroom, and pick up a general park map plus individual maps for day-use and campground areas. The main access sections on the east side of the lake are: (1) White Oak, across the highway from the visitor center, with a day use area often rented to large groups; (2) Crosswinds Campground, adjacent to it

with 182 sites, and including the Crossroads Boating Center and the privately owned Crosswinds Marina with slips and storage- the only place on the lake with a gas dock and pumps; (3) the huge Poplar Point Campground on Beavercreek Road with 579 sites; (4) Ebenezer Church Day-use Area; and (5)New Hope Overlook area near the dam. On the west side of the lake are: (1) Parkers Creek Campground

with 250 sites; (2) the popular Seaforth Day-Use area with a big boat ramp and sandy beaches; (3) Vista Point, smaller in size with a boat ramp, picnic spots, and a group camp area; and (4), the quiet Robeson Creek area, a great place for paddlers off the main channel on Providence Church Road.

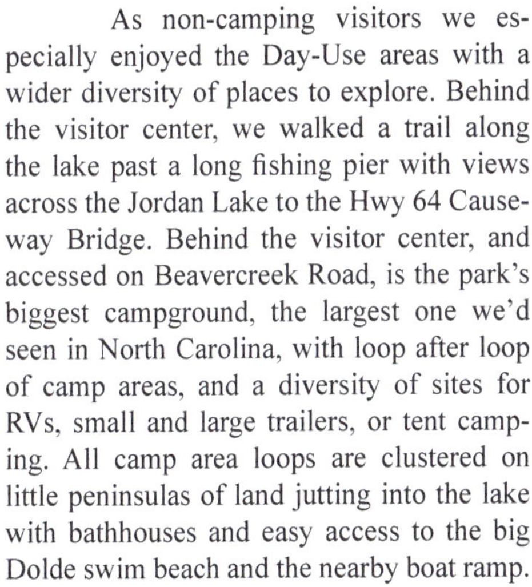

As non-camping visitors we especially enjoyed the Day-Use areas with a wider diversity of places to explore. Behind the visitor center, we walked a trail along the lake past a long fishing pier with views across the Jordan Lake to the Hwy 64 Causeway Bridge. Behind the visitor center, and accessed on Beavercreek Road, is the park's biggest campground, the largest one we'd seen in North Carolina, with loop after loop of camp areas, and a diversity of sites for RVs, small and large trailers, or tent camping. All camp area loops are clustered on little peninsulas of land jutting into the lake with bathhouses and easy access to the big Dolde swim beach and the nearby boat ramp.

We especially liked smaller Parkers Creek Campground to the right just across the Hwy 64 bridge. It had several scenic campground loops on the lake, its own boat ramp, and a 2.25-mile Children's Nature Trail. A second hiking trail loops through the park and connects the campgrounds to the

boat dock and the park's beautiful picnic area and swim beach. Across the road

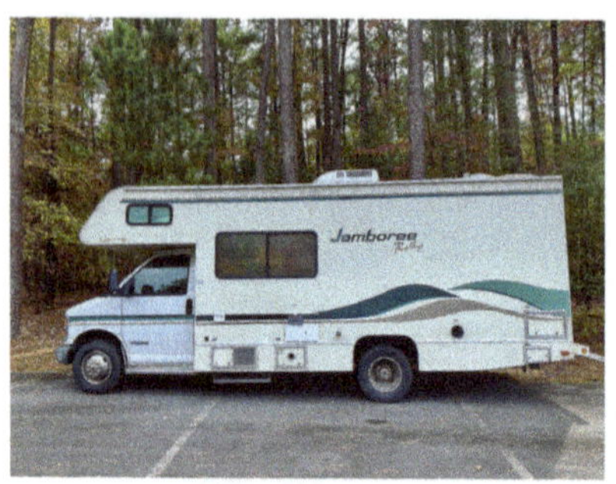

we also loved exploring the popular Seaforth Day Use area. After entering this park section, and not far from the highway, is a huge boat ramp and launch area and large parking lot for trailers and other vehicles. Nearby, by trail or road, were public shower-houses and a small campground area. The Seaforth Pond Trail, a 2-mile loop trail, begins here but can be accessed from several other points along the Seaforth peninsula. The Seaforth Pond Trail passes alongside the lake, through the forest, by ponds and the day-use and picnic areas, and across a long boardwalk in the wetland area. Seaforth has two more small campgrounds with no water & electric, great for tent camping, and several public sites on the water with picnic tables, pavilions, sandy beaches for swimming, plus playgrounds and bathhouses. All were humming with people out enjoying the day, even in October when we visited. This park section was truly an idyllic place to spend a day on the water. J.L. and I had our picnic lunch here before heading back across the causeway bridge again to check out some of the next park sections.

We stopped at Ebenezer Church Day-Use area as we headed south on Beavercreek Road. This recreation area has one of the largest beach fronts on the lake with a playground, shady picnic area and shelters, outdoor showers, and a lovely green lawn. There is also a fine boat dock there and two nice hiking trails, about one mile each. Ebenezer is a good Night-Sky site, too, and rangers and volunteers offer monthly Sky Watching sessions at the recreation area. The New Hope area, beyond Ebenezer on Pea Ridge Road off Beaver Creek, is best known for its hiking trails, the Red Trail and the Blue Trail, the two most challenging in the park. New Hope also has eight boat ramps and 2 launches, a picnic area and some simple camping sites.

Not far away is the B. Everett Jordan Dam, a nice spot to visit, too, managed by the U.S. Army Corps of Engineers. Rangers at the dam sometimes give tours and pedestrians can walk across the dam on one of the area trails. At Poe's

Ridge near the dam is another boat ramp, fishing pier, picnic area, and several trails including the 4.25 mile Poe's Ridge Trail, a challenging loop hike with good views of the lake from the ridgelines. At this busy but diverse park there are enough amenities to keep any visitor entertained in the beauty of the outdoors for days. Put this park on your "don't miss it" list.

Guilford Courthouse National Military Park

Piedmont Region - Guilford County
Park Address: 2332 New Garden Road, Greensboro, NC 27410
Park Size: 250 acres   Month Visited: October
Directions: From Interstate 40 west of Greensboro, turn north on 840/Greensboro Urban Loop. Turn right onto Hwy 220, and then left on New Garden Road, and follow into park.

Park Description:

The Revolutionary War (1775-1783) began over colonial opposition to attempts of the British to impose greater control over the colonies. The battles of the first three years took place primarily in the north but the British then began to move into the South, at first devastating to the Patriots, but the tide began to turn at Cowpens in South Carolina, and the British retreated to North Carolina. At the Battle of Guilford Court House of March 15, 1781, the British Commander Lord Charles Earl Cornwallis's army engaged in battle with Major General Nathanael Greene's militia and army. The battle raged for two hours and over a fourth of Cornwallis's men were killed, wounded, or captured. Although Greene and his forces retreated, Cornwallis's forces, severely damaged, returned to Virginia, and this led to his defeat against George Washington at Yorktown (October 19, 1781), the last battle of the war.

Guilford Courthouse National Military Park became an official national park in 1933 to commemorate this battle, and turning point, in the Revolutionary War. The park protects 250 of the original 1000-acre battlefield. It offers a quiet, reflective place to walk or drive through a scenic park, learning about the battle with the help of informative plaques, signs, and 28 monuments. At the visitor center is a fine museum to explore and the center offers a 30-minute film titled "*Another Such Victory*," telling about the battle and the American and British soldiers involved. You can pick up a map of the battleground and follow the trails exploring the acreage on foot or driving by car around the 2.25-mile tour road. Visitors can access the "Cell Phone Tour" which tells about the battle and sites with a park ranger's narration. The audio is about 38 minutes long and the tour takes about an hour and a half.

The walk through the park is an easy one, but when driving there are well-marked pull-overs leading to the different monuments and commemorative spots along the route. The Nathanael Greene (1742-1786) statue, not far behind the visitor center, is one of the first you will see on the trail. The statue is an impressive bronze one on a granite base, 22 feet tall, with Greene mounted on a stallion. It was interesting to discover that not all the monuments were dedicated to men. Not far from the Greene statue is a tribute figure to Kerenhappuch Turner. She and her husband James were ardent Patriots. James served in the war and Kerenhappuch, a skilled rider, carried dispatches to the Patriots through the British lines and helped with the wounded. Another statue is of Patriot Lt. Colonel Joseph Winston, his hand held high defiantly, who fought in the Battle at Guilford and later served three terms in the U.S. House of Representatives. It was really interesting to tour the park's grounds and to learn not only about the battle but about individuals like Greene, Kerenhappuch,

and Winston who played a role in helping our country attain independence.

Those who want to expand their park visit can also go to the Hoskins Farm, with its historic buildings, only a short walk or drive from the main park. A Farm Cell Phone Tour is available to tell about Joseph and Hannah Hoskins who farmed there. Also, for a lengthier walk, side trails link to adjacent 400-acre Country Park, around the park's lakes, and to the Greensboro Science Center aquarium, museum, and zoo. Locals love this entire park area, tucked right in the middle of a now busy suburban center.

Haw River State Park

Piedmont Region - Rockingham County
Park Address: 339 Conference Center Dr, Browns Summit, NC 27214
Park Size: 1,485 acres   Month Visited: October
Directions: From Interstate 40 west of Greensboro, take I-840 north. Travel to left on 220. Follow to right on 150 east to left on Spearman Road. Continue to park entrance on left.

Park Description:

Fifteen miles north of Greensboro, Haw River is a relatively new member to the NC park system, authorized in 2003 and still developing. The park sits along the banks of the Haw River, which flows 110 miles from its Piedmont headwaters to the Jordan Lake reservoir and into the Cape Fear River. In the past, industries and textile mills on the Haw River heavily polluted the waters. People who swam in the river in those past times would notice their skin taking on the colors of the textile dyes in the water. With pollution and flooding a growing concern, efforts to protect and save the river began within state and local governments. Now the river, safer and more protected, is a natural habitat for fish and wildlife, offers recreational activities, and is the most popular whitewater paddling river in the Piedmont.

The park has two sections, accessible from different parts of the property. The main section, the Summit Environmental Education and Conference Center, was formerly a retreat center owned and operated by the Episcopal Diocese of North Carolina. The Summit has all the main facilities, a park office and lodge, cottages for retreats, 10 cabins, a round house for gatherings, and a full-service dining room in the park lodge. The park, now a residential environmental education center, is still rented to groups and used for training by the park services and it can house over 180 overnight visitors. Around the retreat grounds are recreational facilities, two amphitheaters, a large gymnasium, an outdoor swimming pool, a sports playing field, picnic areas, a disc golf course, and miles of hiking trails.

Several miles of trails wind out of the central area of the Summit. Most begin from a trail behind the park office that travels downhill to the beautiful 6-acre lake on the park's property called Robins Nest Lake. The 0.6-mile Lake Loop Trail winds all around the lake's perimeter and is an easy and pleasant walk.

On the back side of the lake is a boat launch area for canoes and kayaks and on the hill behind the launch is another pavilion and picnic area. Behind this picnic area the 1.4-mile Piedmont Loop Trail begins. This scenic trail weaves its way through a well-maintained, forest path and back to the lakeside again. It also interlinks with the Lake Loop Trail for a longer hike. Near the back of the Piedmont Loop is the short 0.43-mile River Overlook Trail. This is a wetlands trail that winds through a low lying, swamp area on a long boardwalk. The boardwalk is low and close to the water and it travels in and out among the marsh area and flood plain to a small wooden platform and bench overlooking the Haw River. The river is shallow and narrow at this point. You could probably put in a kayak or canoe here but check with the park office for accurate information and to check on the river's status.

The second section of the park, the Iron Ore Belt Access, is not extensively developed yet. A side road off Church Street leads back to a parking area, with a few picnic tables, restrooms, and an informational kiosk. This side of the park lies in the Iron Ore Belt of North Carolina and is near an area where an ironworks facility and furnace operated in the 1770s. A short 0.35-mile connector trail leads from the Iron Ore parking lot to meet the 3.2-mile Great Blue Heron Loop Trail. The trail winds around through the woods, moderately easy to walk unless muddy after extensive rain. Locals especially enjoy this trail.

Mayo River State Park Natural Area

Piedmont Region - Rockingham County
Park Address: 500 Old Mayo Park Road, Mayodan, NC 37027
Park Size: 2,778 acres   Month Visited: October
Directions: From Interstate 40 west of Greensboro, take Interstate 840 North, then left on Hwy 220/311 north. Exit left on Hwy 135 into Mayodan. Take Business 220 north into park property and turn left on Old Mayo Park Road.

Park Description:

Established in 2003, the Mayo River State Park encompasses 2,778 acres of paddlers' access points along the Mayo River. The Mayo River travels from Virginia into North Carolina in two branches that join in Rockingham County near North Carolina's northern border. The river then flows for about 16 miles south to just below the town of Mayodan before joining the Dan River. The park is named after Major William Mayo (1685-1744) an early chief civil engineer in Virginia who helped to survey lands and to set the boundary lines between Virginia and North Carolina. His expedition's surveys provided the first map of the region.

Unlike a traditional state park, Mayo River consists of land sections and access points along the winding river, stretching from the Virginia border to below Mayodan where the river empties into the Dan River. The various property points along the river's route carry names like the Deshazo Mill Access, Anglin Mill Access, Hickory Creek Access, Business 220 Access, and Mayodan Access. At most access points there are few to no facilities, except sometimes a parking area, a picnic table or two, and a paddle access point on the river. Near the Deshazo Mill area at the North Carolina-Virginia border are some of the best rapids on this Class II river section with some Class III rapids. A well-known rapids in this upper area is the Boiling Hole, also a local swimming hole. Off Deshazo Road in the upper park area, is a 1.9-mile trail leading from the road and the Mayo River bank to Fall

Creek waterfall. The broad and tall 15-foot series of falls spills over a rocky embankment into a big pool below.

At the Mayo Mountain Access Point is the park's main area and amenities. The park office is here on a lovely property beside two lakes on a tributary of the Mayo River. There are no camping facilities at this park yet except for a primitive group camp area for organizations

and non-profits off a side road. Although small, the main section of this state park is very scenic with broad, green sweeps of lawn and pretty views across the park's two lakes There is a swim raft in the largest lake, making it a popular spot in summer. Picnic tables sit around the park and on the banks of the lake. The park also has a big pavilion, that can accommodate 100 people, beside the water with an outdoor grill, massive fireplace, and restroom facilities. The lake provides a good spot for fishing and a nice quiet place to enjoy a picnic by the lake. The Mayo Mountain Loop Trail winds its way near the large pavilion, in a loop through the fields, woods, and back again – a good walk popular with the locals. The park also has a flat 0.5-mile Track Trail.

On the road past the main entrance to the park, at the Hwy 220 bridge, is a public canoe access point called the Business 220 Access. Paddlers use this point mostly to get out of the river after a paddle downstream since beyond this point are two dams across the river with no safe portage around or through them. All paddlers should make note of these dams when on the Mayo River and check with the park office about river conditions.

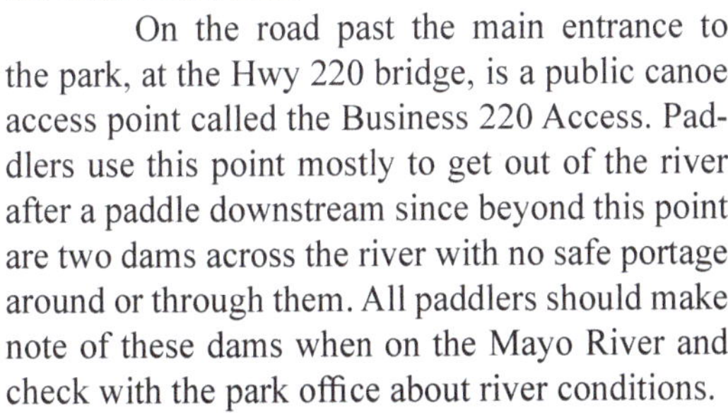

Morrow Mountain State Park Recreation Area

Piedmont Region - Stanly County
Park Address: 49104 Morrow Mtn Road, Albemarle, NC 28001
Park Size: 5,881 acres   Month Visited: October
Directions: From I-40 in Greensboro, take US 220/73 south. Turn right on NC 27/24, traveling west toward Albemarle. Six miles from Albemarle, turn right on Valley Drive and travel three miles. Turn right on Morrow Mountain Road, which leads into the park.

Park Description:

Established in 1939 and located in the Uwharrie Mountains, this park was undoubtedly one of our favorites to visit in the Piedmont. It has a wide diversity of sights to see and amenities to enjoy, including incredible mountain views, camping areas, an Olympic sized swimming pool, museum, amphitheater, over thirty miles of hiking, biking, and equestrian trails, gorgeous river and lake access areas, a boat ramp, boat rentals, scenic picnic areas, pretty pavilions and much more. The mountain and park were named for James McKnight Morrow who donated more than a thousand acres to the park.

Although it's hard to decide where to begin in exploring this lovely park, we'd advise beginning at the attractive Visitor Center. You can get a good park map here and walk through the parking lot to visit Morrow Mountain's interest-

ing museum. We enjoyed learning about the area's history and ecology, seeing photos of the park's early years, and watching the informative videos.

A side road near the visitor center led to the park's six rental cabins and another nearby road led into the shady, attractive family campground area. There are 106 well-spaced campsites for RV, trailer and tent camping with bathhouses, electric hookup and a dump station. The park also has a nice group camp area near the river and a remote primitive camping site. Near the campground road on another side street is an Olympic-sized pool, tennis courts, a playing field, bathhouse, and recreation center. One of the park's trails, the Hattaway Mountain trail begins by the pool, a two-mile strenuous one and another trail leads over to the campground.

Further down the road from the pool is a large parking lot with picnic tables and pavilions scattered around the grounds in shady spots. Several other park trails begin at this area, including an interesting and easy 0.6-mile Quarry Trail. It passes by an old quarry the Civilian Conservation Corps took rock from to build many of the park's buildings, walls, and bridges.

We drove on next to the Pee Dee River and Lake Tillery with beautiful vistas out across the water, a boat ramp, boat rentals, more picnic tables, and the beginnings of two more nice trails. A scenic boardwalk leads from the boat ramp to the large parking lot for cars and trailers where a fine wooden fishing pier reaches out into the river. The beginning of the 4.1-mile Fall Mountain Trail leads along the shore to a boat rental and concessions building before looping to the group camp area and back through the forest again. Also the easy 0.8-mile Three Rivers Trail, known for wildflowers in the spring, starts near the boat ramp and winds in a loop to a ridgetop and back. This area is a great spot for fishing, boating, canoeing, and kayaking.

After leaving the river, we took a fork off the main road to drive to the historic Kron house and property. At the end of the road, a trail leads up wooden stairs to the historic cabin and buildings on the hillside. The home belonged to Dr. Francis Kron, one of the Piedmont's famous doctors and a noted horticulturist. His home, greenhouse, and infirmary remain much as they looked in the 1800s. Dr. Kron and his wife had two daughters and both lived on at the homesite until they died. A garden plot and small graveyard sits behind the property, and informative kiosks tell the history about this remarkable man and his family who gave their land to the park.

Keep in mind, while exploring the park, that artifacts found in the area suggest that Native American Indians lived and hunted here 12,000 years before European settlers. An old ferry, Lowder's Ferry, used to operate on the river and many of the park's buildings were made with argillite rock mined on the park site

in earlier years. The park property is also latticed with many fine trails for horseback riding, and near the beginning of the park is an Equestrian Parking Area where three popular riding trails begin.

One of the highlights of this park is Morrow Mountain itself. Before leaving the park, take the long winding road to the top of the mountain where you'll find several overlooks and benches where you can stand or sit to look out over stunning panoramas. The summit of the mountain is 936 feet high and on a clear day you'll enjoy superb views across the surrounding countryside. A covered picnic table sits up a short pathway from the parking lot, along with picnic tables on a scenic hillside. The short 0.8-mile Mountain Loop Trail links around the top of the mountain and the longer and steeper 2.6-mile Morrow Mountain Trail also begins here. A day is almost not enough time to enjoy all the amenities in this fine park.

Hanging Rock State Park Recreation Area

Park Address: 1790 Hanging Rock Park Road, Danbury, NC 27016
Park Size: 9,011 acres   Month Visited: October
Directions: From I-40 in Winston-Salem take US 52 north to right on NC Hwy 8. Follow to left on Hwy 89 to Danbury and turn left on Hanging Rock Road/Hwy 2015 into the park.

Park Description:

Thirty miles north of Winston-Salem, the Hanging Rock State Park protects the high peaks in the Sauratown Mountain Range, many rising 1,700 feet above the surrounding Piedmont. Purchased by the state in 1935, the park is full of immense quartzite rock formations, crags, sheer cliffs, and deep ravines, all set in the midst of a parkland rich with rolling hills, lovely forests, lakes, streams, and waterfalls. Many of the buildings, trails, picnic areas, the old bathhouse, and the stone dam across the lake were constructed by the Civilian Conservation Corps (CCC) between 1935 and 1942. In addition to 48 miles of hiking trails, plus biking and equestrian trails, this scenic park offers campgrounds, fishing, rock climbing, a swim lake, boat rentals, picnic areas, an amphitheater, and much more.

It would take more than a day to explore every aspect of this park and hike all of its trails, but the best place to begin an initial tour is at the new visitor center. Enjoy the exhibits there and pick up maps and brochures about the park's campgrounds, cabins, and trails. Just across from the visitor center parking lot is the beginning of the 1.3-miles (2.6-mi RT) Hanging Rock Trail, one of the park's most popular walks. The trail is moderate in the early section and grows more strenuous as it rises up a series of rock stairs, and through a jumble of rocks, boulders and ledges, to reach its end and highest points. The Hanging Rock, a rough quartzite formation, juts out from the summit's peak at

2,159 feet, and many visitors climb out onto the rock to sit and enjoy the stunning views of the valley and park. For most visitors, the roundtrip hike is a challenge, even for the physically fit, taking about two hours to complete.

If you like trails to waterfalls there are two more trails beginning near the visitor center you might enjoy. The easier 0.2-mile trail to Cascades Falls begins from the 0.1-mile Rock Garden Trail by the center and leads to a long bridge and wooden overlook where you can see the falls tumbling down a rocky hillside. A more strenuous trail nearby is the Indian Creek Trail leading to two scenic waterfalls, Hidden Falls at 0.4 mile and Widow Falls at 0.6 mile. Both require climbs down steep rocky ledges and stairs but the waterfalls are pretty to see and the pathway passes by a picnic pavilion and restrooms. The entire Indian Creek Trail is 3.6 miles, leading

all the way to the Dan River at the back of the park, but the section to both falls and back is only two miles.

After enjoying a hike, head down the road to the park's 12-acre lake. A big fishing pier reaches out into the water and benches sit around the lake shore, good spots for fishing or just dreaming and resting. Trails wind in and out around the lake, and across the old dam built by the CCC, and pavilions and picnic areas sit on the shaded hillsides above the lakeside. One trail leads to the old rock bathhouse and concessions building toward the southern end of the lake where you'll find a fine sand beach and swim area, boat rentals, and an old historic boat house.

A side trail from the lake leads directly over to the park's main campground. Hanging Rock's family campground spreads around the end of a quiet loop road. On a winding street nearby, you'll also find ten rustic cabins on picturesque sites. There is also a group camp nearer the visitor center off the Indian Creek Trail. The main family campground has 73 non-electric tent/trailer sites but no RV or trailer hookups. It also offers a dump station, two bathhouses with hot showers, a recycling bin, and an amphitheater. All the

spacious campsites sit on a shady road.

Hanging Rock Park is a hiker's paradise and, if you have time, there are many interesting trails to hike and enjoy. One is the 4.7-mile (9.4 mi RT) Moore's Wall Loop. It's a challenging hike, and a steep climb, with lots of rock stairs, but the trail leads to two interesting points, the Balancing Rock and Moore's Knob Overlook Tower. Near

the summit a spur trail branches off to reach Balanced Rock, a big chunk of quartzite sitting on a rock base like a giant ship's hull balanced precariously on a rock. Further on a set of steep stairs winds to the lookout tower at 2,560-feet. You can climb the tower stairs to see tremendous views in every direction. Another trail, Crook's Wall Trail, a strenuous 2.2-mile (4.4 mi RT) hike, leads to more high vistas, like the rocky Crook's Wall, with scenic overlooks, and the tall crag called the House Rock.

Outside the central section of the park, Hall Road on the north leads to two more places to explore that don't require a long, taxing hike. The first scenic spot is a pretty 35-foot waterfall at the end of the 0.4-mile Lower Cascades Trail. Continuing west on Hall Road, left on Mickey Road, and then left again on Charlie Young Road leads to the parking lot to Tory's Cave and Falls – only about five miles from the main park entrance. A short, less than a half mile trail leads right to Tory's Den, an incredible 30-foot rock cave said to have been a Tories' hideout in the Revolutionary War. To the left a second short walk leads to a rocky outcrop where you can see Tory Falls spilling over some tall rocky bluffs. Hanging Rock State Park is truly a stunner overall, so put this park on your "must visit" list.

Lake Norman State Park

Piedmont Region - Iredell County
Park Address: 759 State Park Road, Troutman, NC 28166
Park Size: 1,328 acres   Month Visited: May
Directions: From I-40 west of Statesville, take Hwy 64-70, Garner Bagmal Blvd south. Follow to right/south on Hwy 21 south. Continue to Troutman and turn right on Wagner St/Perth Road, turning right on State Park Road and follow into the park.

Park Description:

Lake Norman State Park is another of North Carolina's beautiful lakeside parks. It sits on Lake Norman, one of the largest manmade lakes in the state, which covers over 323,000 acres with a shoreline of 520 miles in total and is nicknamed "the Inland Sea." Seventeen miles of that shoreline are in Lake Norman State Park and it also has its own private lake within it. The park opened in 1962 after the Duke Power Company built the Cowans Ford Dam across the Catawba, to generate electrical energy, and gave land for a park to the state of North Carolina. The park offers a host of amenities for visitors to enjoy—campgrounds, a public swim beach, hiking and biking trails, picnic areas and pavilions, a community building, a boat ramp, fishing pier, and more in a spectacular, scenic location.

The main entry road winds into the park's acreage and passes a side road and access points to a network of wonderful bike trails, before crossing a short bridge and coming to the large visitor center and park office. Inside are a host of exhibits about the park and its history, as well as meeting rooms. Behind the office lies 13-acre Park Lake with a scenic, winding trail along its banks and pretty picnic sites and pavilions near the water. Kayaks, canoes, pedal boats, or stand-up paddleboards can be rented to use on the lake and several of the park's hiking

trails begin here also.

The 0.9-mile Alder Trail winds from behind the parking lot to loop around a peninsula in the lake. A side trail leads over to the dam and the trail is an easy one for all ages, taking about 20 minutes to walk. The short Dragonfly 0.25-mile loop trail is also great for kids with interactive educational exhibits along its way. It is paved and also wheelchair accessible.

Across the road from the visitor center is one of the most loved biking trails, the Itusi trail, named in tribute to the Catawba Indians who used to live around this area long ago. The full Itusi is 30.5 miles, consisting of several other shorter trails linking together. Hikers can also enjoy this, and other bike trails, but are expected to yield for bikers. At the visitor center, riders can pick up a map showing

the locations of the biking trails. Each of the bike trails can be ridden separately

and some can be linked for longer rides.

Continuing on the main road west from the Visitor Center leads to a turn on Group Camp Lane to a group camp on the water and a large community building that can be rented for events. The long 5.2-mile Lakeshore Trail can be accessed from this parking area by a spur trail but can also be accessed from several other areas in the park. It takes about two hours to hike all of the trail, which weaves in and out along the lakesides and hikers will find rest benches along its route.

Not far down the road from the turn to the group camp and community building, Boat Launch Drive turns east to lead down to the park's fine boat launch area. All boats can launch free from this site to spend the day on the water. Fishing is very popular at Lake Norman and several fishing tournaments are held on the lake every year. Anglers catch striped, spotted, and largemouth bass, bluegill, crappie, and yellow perch. Across the road down Shortleaf Drive is a long fishing pier, also popular with anglers.

Shortleaf Drive also leads to the park's swim beach. This is a 125-yard-long sand beach with picnic tables and pavilions nearby. Above the beach is a big boathouse with lockers and showers and a concessions area. The beach at Lake Norman is always busy in the warm months and popular for all ages. When lifeguards are present in summer the park

charges a small fee to swim but otherwise the beach is free.

Off nearby Family Camp Circle is the park's campground. It has 33 campsites for tents or trailer camping, bathhouses, and a dump station. Some sites are good for RVs but the campground has no hookups. The campground sites are on a shaded loop road on a finger of the lake within walking distance to the water and to the Lakeshore Trail. In addition, the park has recently built and opened six new rental cabins. The cabins have two rooms each with water, sewer, and electricity and a bathhouse and restrooms nearby.

For water enthusiasts Lake Norman is a wonderful park to visit. Additionally it is only ten miles south of Statesville to other historic and scenic

spots, like the Fort Dobbs Historic Site in Statesville, Murray's Mill in Catawba, and Zootastic Park in Troutman.

Crowders Mountain State Park

Piedmont Region - Gaston County
Park Address: 522 Park Office Lane, Gastonia, NC 28952
Park Size: 5,300 acres   Month Visited: May
Directions: From I-85, take Hwy 321 South at Gastonia. Turn right/East on Hwy 74. Follow to left on Sparrow Springs Road/ State Rd # 1125. Continue on Sparrow Springs into park. Turn right on State Park Lane and then right on Park Office Lane to main visitor center.

Park Description:

The main attraction at Crowders State Park are its high, craggy peaks and many hiking trails. The park is named for Crowders Mountain that rises more than 800 feet above the surrounding Piedmont. Scientists call the mountain range here an erosional remnant left over from a prehistoric mountain range formed millions of years ago. Despite its high mountain ranges, Crowders Mountain State Park is a surprisingly dry state park without the usual rushing creeks, cascades, and falls associated with mountain peaks. The park first opened in the 1970s, adding more acreage later to first take in the Pinnacle and then a section of land connecting the park to Kings Mountain State Park and Kings Mountain National Military Park across the border in South Carolina.

The park's visitor center lies in a valley between the two peaks the park is best known for—Crowders Mountain, at 1,625 feet, and The Pinnacle, at 1,705 feet. At the visitor center, you'll find an exhibit hall display and a relief map of the park. The center is also the best location to pick up needed maps and information about the trails and trail conditions. With a permit, rope climbing is also allowed in certain areas of the park. Crowders has few amenities and no camping facilities except backcountry, primitive sites and a group camp.

Next to the visitor center is the park's beautiful nine-acre lake, a very scenic spot. A small side road beside it leads to the picnic area, with a multitude of appealing tables scattered near the lake's shores and two nice shelters. Canoes can be rented at the park office but swimming and private boats are not permitted. However, fishing for bass and bream is enjoyed along the lake's shoreline. Two easy trails, a pleasure for all to enjoy, begin from this area, the 0.8-mile Fern Trail starting at the picnic shelter and the almost one-mile Lake Trail that loops around the lake.

The Lake Trail starts near the pretty fishing pier by the lake side, passes through a small bog over a foot bridge, and has rest benches along the way. Another trail called the Turnback Trail leads for 1.2 miles on a moderate hike to the Pinnacle Trail, and is often the turn-around point before the trail begins to grow steeper and more difficult.

Behind the visitors center, Crowders Mountain Trail leads northeast toward Crowders Mountain, and the Pinnacle Trail leads southwest to the Pinnacle. The approximately 2-miles (or 4-miles RT) Pinnacle Trail travels steeply on a challenging route to high rocky bluffs and overlooks and takes about two hours to hike. The Crowders Mountain Trail is an equally strenuous approximately 3 miles (or 6-miles RT) hike climbing to the top of Crowders Mountain to reach an overlook and rugged cliffs that offer spectacular views for many miles. This hike takes about three hours. Several other trails lead to the top of Crowders Mountain, the Rocktop Trail, 2.5-miles in length, noted as especially difficult and challenging, and two trails from the northeast Linwood Road Access in the park, the 1.8-mile gravel Tower Trail and the vertical 0.8-mile Backside Trail that climbs the mountain's back with 336 stairs. For all these trails to the peaks, good hiking shoes and gear, and good physical fitness, are advised.

Stone Mountain

MOUNTAINS REGION STATE PARK INDEX

Pilot Mountain State Park 132

New River State Park 136

Mount Jefferson State Park 138

Stone Mountain State Park 140

Elk Knob State Park 144

South Mountains State Park 146

Lake James State Park 148

Overmountain Victory National Historic Park 152

Blue Ridge Parkway National Parkway 154

Mount Mitchell State Park 158

Grandfather Mountain State Park 160

Carl Sandburg National Historic Site 164

Chimney Rock State Park 166

Appalachian National Scenic Trail 170

Rendezvous Mountain State Park 172

Trail of Tears National Historic Trail 174

Gorges State Park 176

Great Smoky Mountains National Park 180

Mountains Region
North Carolina PARKS

Chimney Rock

Mount Mitchell

Lake James

Pilot Mountain

Pilot Mountain State Park Recreation Area

Mountains Region - Surry & Yadkin County
Park Address: 1792 Pilot Knob Park Road, Pinnacle. NC 27043
Park Size: 3,782 acres   Month Visited: October
Directions: From I-40, take I-77 north. Turn east on I-74 toward White Plains and then right and south on Hwy 52, Pilot Mountain Pkwy. Continue to state park entrance on right.

Park Description:

Only 14 miles south of Mt Airy and not far from the Virginia/North Carolina state line, Pilot Mountain, a granite stone hill or monadnock, stands 2,421 feet high, rising far above the Piedmont landscape around it. This solitary knob is the centerpiece of the park and was dedicated as a National Natural Landmark in 1976. The Saura Indians, who once lived in these mountains, called the towering stone hill Jomeokee, meaning the Pilot or Great Guide, and that's where the mountain and park got its name. The land was originally mapped in 1751 by a team of geographers that included the father of Thomas Jefferson. Pilot Mountain was a commercial tourist attraction for many years but became the state's 14th park in 1968.

On the road leading into the park, swing left to first visit the big new visitor center on the hillside. It has a fine exhibit area and is the best place to learn about the park, its sections, and amenities. Across from the visitor center are the beginnings, or access points, to several of the park's lower level hiking trails. The Grindstone Trail, a strenuous hike, climbs from the center up the mountain

and to the top of the pinnacle. Heading west on flatter ground is the 1.5-mile Grassy Ridge Trail. We walked a portion of this trail, weaving through a grassy meadow back into the woods and then returning on the 0.4-mile Fiddlehead Trail it intersects. From the field we could see fine views of Pilot Mountain in the distance. The park has over 24 miles of hiking trails, from easy or moderate to steep and strenuous ones. In the fall, migrating birds come through the park, including over a dozen species of raptors like broad-winged hawks and Cooper's hawks. Additionally, ravens like nesting in these high mountains and you may see them soaring above the peaks.

After leaving the visitor center, take the long winding road up to the summit of Pilot Mountain. It reminded us of the roads in the Smoky Mountains near our home, ending at the big Jacob Fork parking lot high on the peak's top. Several

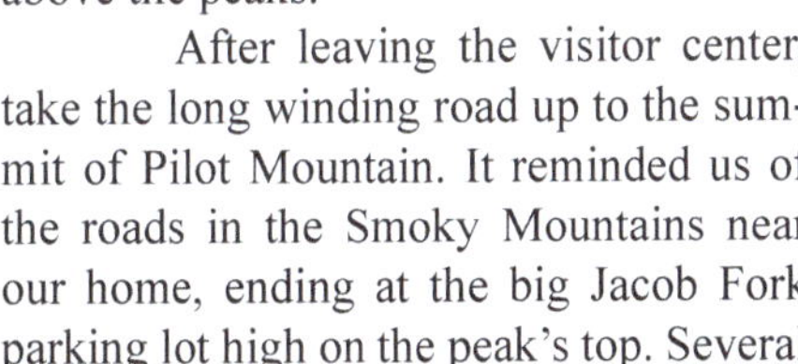

trails wind out from the parking area but our first choice was the short Little Pinnacle Overlook Trail which led for less than a half mile up a rocky path to a fine overlook of the distinctive Big Pinnacle of Pilot Mountain at the top. Along the way are several other overlooks where you can enjoy stunning views across the surrounding area far below. Another trail, the Sassafras Trail, winds around the eastern base of the summit for different views.

Back at the parking lot is a large wooden viewing area, offering more panoramic views across the hills, valleys, farms, and towns below. A paved side trail, with benches along its route, leads from the viewing platform to a shady, inviting picnic area with benches, grills, nearby restrooms, and a large pavilion that can be reserved. Beyond the picnic area are connections to other steeper and more strenuous trails and to a rock-climbing area. One trail circles the base of the pinnacle and provides views of the rocky cliffs from different perspectives.

On the way back down the mountain we checked out the park's campground on a shady, paved side road. The campground has 49 campsites for trailers or tents and a bathhouse. All sites have a grill, tent pad and picnic table. An amphitheater sits near the park entrance for ranger talks and two trails wind out of the campground area.

The park has two other sections centering along the Yadkin River to the south. These sections, more remote, are especially popular with paddlers and equestrians. To access the Bean Shoals area, leave the main park area and travel south on the highway to the first right at Pinnacle Hotel Road. Follow into Hauser Road and to the access road on the left at the park sign. An unpaved road leads down to the river. The road has three drive-through stream crossings and no bridges and may not be suitable for all vehicles, especially when streams are high. At the end of the road is access to the river and to the Yadkin Islands Hiking Trail. Along the river are the rock wall remains of the Bean Shoals Canal, started in the 1800s but never finished. Across the river, reached by a different road, is the Ivy Bluff Access area, with a boat access point and primitive campground. Continuing further up Hauser Road leads to an equestrian parking lot, where several horse trails begin, and across the street is the 6.6-mile corridor trail leading over to the main park.

Adjacent to this southern park section is the Horne Creek Living Historical Farm, managed by the state of North Carolina. It is not officially a part of the park property but is a delight to visit, depicting farm life in the early 1900s. A winding road leads back to a visitor center, museum, and gift shop where you can get a map of the farm property. Another road leads back to the farm site and the pretty, white two-storied Hauser farm home, fields, barns, corn crib, orchard, garden, and sheds. Be sure to add a visit to this farm to your park day.

New River State Park

Mountains Region - Ashe & Alleghany County
Park Address: 358 New River State Park Rd, Laurel Springs, NC 28644
Park Size: 3,323 acres   Month Visited: October
Directions: From Boone, NC, follow Hwy 421 east and turn left on Hwy 221. Follow Hwy 221 north through Jefferson to park entrance on right before the New River Bridge crossing.

Park Description:

Starting in Ashe County in North Carolina, and touching into Alleghany County, the New River stretches 320 miles, reaching into Virginia and West Virginia. The winding river is considered to be one of the five oldest rivers in the world and in 1976 was declared a part of the National Wild and Scenic River System. A long 26.5-mile piece of river, and the seven access points along its route, are protected by the NC state park system. The New River is a paddlers' paradise for canoeing, kayaking, and tubing. Fishing is also good on the river and many of the park's access areas have hiking trails, picnic areas, and primitive camp sites.

The main section of the state park is at the U.S. 221 Access Area, off Hwy 221, not far from Jefferson. All the information you need about the park, its sections, camping, and river conditions are available at the main park office. The office and visitor center is a beautiful facility with meeting rooms, an exhibit area, and a broad deck with picnic tables on the back. One of New River's trails, a short Track Trail, begins behind the park office. Near the visitor center is a new camping area for tent, trailer, or RV camping with restrooms and a bathhouse. This park section also has a paddle-in camp and a group camp with a bathhouse and restrooms.

Down the main road, leading toward the river, is a picnic area and large pavilion on a hillside. The Dogwood Trail leads from behind the pavilion to an

136

overlook with a kiosk and rest bench. A nice Community Building sits off the main road, too, with facilities for group meetings. At the end of the main road is another parking lot with access to the river for kayaks or canoes. Scenic benches sit along the water, and a side road leads back into the second campground. The 1.2-mi Hickory Trail winds from the parking lot back to the visitor

center, a pretty woods trail and a pleasant walk with black-eyed Susans along the trailside and wildflowers in summer. Also, the River Run Trail winds from the lower parking area to follow through a pine forest and hardwood forest to the old Stump Homestead. The Stump Family farmed here from the late 1930s through much of the 1950s and the chimney of their old home, some fencing, a spring house and root cellar still sit on the property.

The only other park sections with road access are Wagoner and Elk Shoals. The Wagoner area to the south has a campground, picnic areas and a paddle access point, while the smaller Elk Shoals area is known for tubing and its swim beach. The other access points are canoe in only—Alleghany, Prathers Creek, and Riverbend. These sites have only primitive campgrounds, no restrooms, a few picnic tables, and a parking area for paddle access.

The New River is an easy river for all abilities to paddle and a good river for beginners. The river is mostly gentle and shallow but with a current that carries the canoe without as much paddling. This river travels north instead of south, so keep that fact in mind with boat trip planning. If you didn't bring, or don't have, your own canoe, kayak or tube, Little River Outfitters in nearby Jefferson rents them and also offers guided 2-3-hour canoeing and kayaking trips.

Mount Jefferson State Park Natural Area

Mountains Region - Ashe County
Park Address: 358 New River Road, Laurel Springs, NC 28644
Park Size: 3,323acres   Month Visited: October
Directions: From Boone, NC, follow Hwy 421 east and turn left on Hwy 221. Follow Hwy 221 north. Cross Hwy 163 and turn right in West Jefferson on Hwy 1153/State Park Road.

Park Description:

Mount Jefferson was named in 1952 for President Thomas Jefferson and for his father Peter Jefferson who owned and surveyed the land in the 1700s. You might think of Mount Jefferson as "the park that almost didn't become a park." Early efforts to get the land on top of Mount Jefferson to be designated as a state park failed because the park lacked the minimum acreage to be adopted as a park. However, area citizens worked hard to get the additional land needed and Mount Jefferson became a State Park Natural Area in 1956. In 1974 it was also designated as a National Natural Landmark because of its ecological diversity.

The peak of Mount Jefferson, its summit at 4,683 feet, rises more than a thousand feet above the surrounding town and land below it. Its black metamorphic rock gives the peak its dark appearance. Mount Jefferson was once a part of a mighty mountain range but time and erosion have worn it down. The area is rich with history, and legends say Mount Jefferson's ledges served as hideouts for escaped slaves traveling the Underground Railroad.

The entry road into the park winds for 3.6 miles up a narrow road, at first through a populated town area but eventually reaching a small park office and utility area on the left. There are no stops, pullovers, or points of interest along the way. Note the park office is often unattended with no pickup area for park brochures and maps so you might want to print a map to bring with you. Across from the office is the entry point for one of the park's trails, the new 2-mile one way (4 mi RT) Mountain Ridge Trail that winds steeply through the forest almost parallel to the park road and up to the Summit and picnic area. It passes two overlooks on its way, both of which can also be reached by car.

The first overlook on the route to the Summit is the Sunrise Overlook with fine vistas to the west across West Jefferson and the valley below. The nearby Sunset Overlook can be accessed by a 0.3-mile Spur Trail. The steep ongoing road north arrives next at the Jefferson Overlook, a pullover and rocky outcropping on the mountain top with stunning views to the west and north. On a clear day you can see for miles and miles. Continuing on leads to Mount Jefferson's Summit and a large parking area. There is a picnic area, restrooms, and a fine covered pavilion here, offering more memorable views from the top of the mountain. In October when we visited, the foliage was particularly pretty.

Several trails, interlinking, reach out from the Summit. The Summit Trail, a short 0.3-mile strenuous trail starts at the parking area to walk to Mount Jefferson's summit, passing by a tower and power lines before reaching the trail's high point. From this point the Rhododendron Trail travels 1.1 miles out along the ridge to Luther Rock with more good views of the valley and towns below before looping back. Another trail, the Lost Province Trail, a more moderate 0.75-mile trail, leads off the Rhododendron Trail through a nice forest area but with no overlook views. The rest of the park is a wilderness natural area, protecting the plants and animals that call this area home. For a park with camping and more amenities, New River State Park is only 14 miles north off Hwy 221.

Stone Mountain State Park

Mountains Region - Alleghany & Wilkes County
Park Address: 3042 Frank Parkway, Roaring Gap, NC 28668
Park Size: 14,353 acres   Month Visited: October
Directions: From I-40 turn north on I-77 North, turn left/west on
Hwy 21 at Elkin. Follow to left on Traphill Rd/State Rd 1002.
Continue on right/north on John P. Frank Parkway into park.

Park Description:

     As you enter the Stone Mountain park you soon see glimpses of the 600-foot high dome-shaped granite mountain that is the centerpiece of this large park and a National Natural Landmark. It rises 600 feet from its base, is over four miles in circumference, and stands at 2,305 feet above sea level. We really enjoyed visiting this park as it has a wonderful diversity and a lot to see and do, with miles of hiking trails, camping, picnicking, trout streams, waterfalls and cascades, and historic sites, all in a panoramic setting. In the Park Office is a Mountain Culture Exhibit, telling the park's history and how early settlers lived. There are also scenic wildlife displays, like an incredible collection of butterflies and moths. Be sure to pick up a park map here to help you find your way around this widespread park.

     Our first stop was to turn off the main road on Royal Camp Lane to drive through the large family campground area, with several loop roads winding along Big Sandy Creek. The campground has 90 campsites for tents, trailers, and rec-

reational vehicles, electric and water hookups, bathhouses, and a dump station. Only Loop A, with 37 sites, is designated for tent camping only. The park also has a group camp and a primitive tent camp area in another section of the park.

Not far away from the campground and visitor center is a large picnic area with many tables and shelters. An 0.75-mile Connector Trail leads out from this area to connect with the south end of the Stone Mountain Loop Trail. The moderate trail twines through the woods and along the Creekside

to an old rock chimney and a split in the pathway. To the right you can hike about two miles on the summit side of the Stone Mountain Loop Trail to reach the top of Stone Mountain and walk out on top of it. There are tremendous views here for miles across the surrounding area, and you can rest on the mountain top and enjoy them before returning.

If you take the left fork at the chimney site, which we did, the trail leads to an overlook at the top of Stone Mountain Falls (known locally as Beauty Falls).

This spectacular waterfall cascades over a series of stone bluffs for 200 feet before ending in a large pool below. From the overlook, you can peek over the fencing to see the big falls plunging over the mountain, but to really see it, you need to climb down the long length of 300 wooden stairs to the bottom where you can look up and catch the best view of this stunning falls. There are rest benches along the way, well needed for this rather heart-pumping climb down or up.

At the bottom of the falls, you can opt to walk back to your car, or hike on further along Stone Mountain Trail. We returned to our car and then followed the park road to the next parking lot to hike a portion of the Stone Mountain Loop Trail from its other end. The trail wove through a forested area, climbing in and out around ledges and a creek to arrive at a kiosk and side trail leading to the Hutchinson Homestead. This old farm was built in the 19th century and the buildings later restored by the park so tourists could see and imagine life in these mountains in that past time. The farmstead area has a log cabin, barn, corn crib, fenced garden plot, blacksmith shop, and other side buildings on a pretty site with Stone Mountain rising high behind it.

Other trails from out of the same parking area wind to the summit of the

mountain or link into more trails winding to other rocky points like Wolf Rock and Cedar Rock Trail. The entire Stone Mountain Loop Trail, traveling from the parking area and across the summit to return again is 4.5-miles in length and a strenuous workout. Another trail leads off the Stone Mountain Loop Trail to reach two other waterfalls, Middle Falls and Lower Falls. If you're camping or staying in the area for several days, there are hiking trails throughout the park to explore and enjoy as well as equestrian trails.

A final spot not to miss while visiting the park is a hike to Widow's Falls. The entire trail is 2.5 miles but it's only about a half mile to the falls, a scenic and idyllic spot. Nearby are many fine spots for anglers on the East Prong of the Roaring River. The park offers 17 miles of trout streams, and fishing is very popular here. Our last stop, down the road from the falls, was at the historic Garden Creek Baptist Church, established in 1897. It is one of the oldest churches in the area and still has services on Sundays. A little cemetery

with old graves lies up the hill from the church. We both wished we'd had more time to hike more trails and explore more sites in this beautiful park, and it is one we'd really like to visit again.

Elk Knob State Park Natural Area

Mountains Region - Watauga County
Park Address: 5564 Meat Camp Road, Todd, NC 28644
Park Size: 4,423acres   Month Visited: October
Directions: From Boone NC, follow Hwy 421 east and turn left on Hwy 194 north. Turn left after 4-miles on Meat Camp Road/Hwy 1340 which leads in 5-miles to park entrance on right.

Park Description:

Elk Knob State Park was established in 2003 to preserve the unique area around Elk Knob, one of the highest peaks in Watauga County, and to help protect the headwaters of the New River, one of the oldest rivers, not only in the US but in the world. The park's Elk Knob name was inspired by the elk that once wandered the area in the 1700s. There are no elk today but there are a diverse variety of wildlife, trees, plants, and flowers. We enjoyed the fall beauty of the trees on our October visit and even spotted late wildflowers still in bloom. On a side note, the name Meat Camp refers to the unincorporated community around the park, which got its name from an early meat packing house used by hunters before the Revolutionary War. The Meat Camp area around Elk Knob is rich in history, once a thriving community with grist mills and settlers. Every September the park promotes a Community Day event for locals and tourists to enjoy, with old craft demonstrations, history remembrances, storytelling, and music.

The park has limited amenities but it is rich with natural scenery. There is a small visitor center, a picnic area on a quiet loop road, an amphitheater, a few primitive backcountry campsites, scenic hiking trails, and skiing opportunities in the winter.

Hiking is the main attraction at Elk Knob and there are four trails to enjoy. One is the easy one-mile Beech Tree Trail, or Kids Track Trail, that links around the back of the picnic area through a beech forest. Colorful signs along the way help kids identify plants and

flowers they might see. The half mile Maple Tree Run, reaches out from the amphitheater area, almost paralleling the main park road. The park's most popular hike is the 1.9-mile (appx.4 mi RT) Summit Trail, a gradual steep climb up through the woods to reach two high Elk Knob overlooks. The trail, once an old loggers' road, rises 1,000 feet to two panoramic views of the hills and valleys below. The peak at Elk Knob sits at an elevation of 5,520 feet and is the third highest peak in the county. On a clear day you can see all the way to far-away peaks like Bluff Mountain, Mount Jefferson, Grandfather Mountain, and Snake Mountain—especially pretty in the fall. The park's other trail, the long 3.8-mi Backcountry Trail, winds east from the parking area to a backcountry group camp and to several primitive tent camping sites.

In the winter months snowshoeing and cross-country skiing are popular at the park. Cross-country skiing is best on the Beech Tree Trail and the shorter Maple Run Trail. Even though the park is only 10-11 miles above Boone, be aware that a four-wheel drive vehicle might be necessary to access the park in snow and ice conditions.

Elk Knob is one of the state's newer parks and it has plans to expand and to add more property and amenities. The park hopes to build a new and larger visitor center, to create a camping area, and to add pavilions and more hiking trails. An additional plus for the park is its short proximity to Boone and Blowing Rock where visitors can enjoy a variety of other sites while in the area.

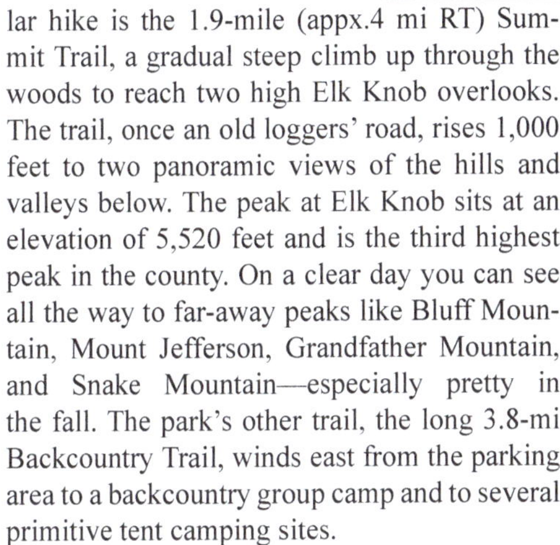

South Mountains State Park

Mountains Region - Burke County
Park Address: 3001 State Park Ave, Connelly Springs, NC 28612
Park Size: 20,000+ acres   Month Visited: May
Directions: From I-40 just east of Salem, take Hwy 18 south. Continue south and then right on Old North Carolina 18 Road. Follow to left on Ward Gap Road and then right into South Mountains Park Road and into the Jacob Fork Access of the park.

Park Description:

The largest park in North Carolina, South Mountains State Park, sprawls over more than 20,000 acres of rugged terrain. The Jacob Fork Access leads into the main area of the park, to the park office and visitor center, and to the primary park amenities. Although the bulk of the park is predominantly wilderness terrain, visitors can enjoy 50 miles of hiking trails, 35 miles of equestrian trails, and 17 miles of bike trails. The park also offers picnic areas, primitive campgrounds, and an amphitheater. Visitors will find cascades and waterfalls, an abundance of rushing streams to trout fish in, rocky cliffs, spectacular high point views, deep forests, a diverse array of wildlife, 60 species of birds, and beautiful wildflowers in spring and summer. The park is an outdoor lovers' paradise, away from the busy, hectic world, but not far from metropolitan areas.

To touch on the park's history, the Catawba and Cherokee Indians once hunted and fought here. Settlers came to the area as early as the late 1700s and gold was found in 1828, creating a frantic "gold rush" for a time. Timber companies later moved in, cutting over 26,000 acres before the state established the South Mountains Wildlife Management area and established the park in the 1970s.

Day visitors usually enjoy hiking some of the park's more accessible and easier trails. The most family friendly, is the 0.25-mile Hemlock Nature Trail, an easy trail with eleven displays along the way, which starts at the Jacobs Fork parking lot at the end of the road beyond the visitor center. The 0.5-mile easy River Trail begins here, too, and winds along the border of Jacob Fork River, fun for kids and adults. The 1.5-mile Hidden Cove Trail is a pleasant, easy to moderate woods trail, starting about a mile from the visitor center on the left. Near these trails are the

park's picnic areas, pavilions, and restrooms, with easy access to the trailheads.

For more veteran hikers, the most popular trail in the park is High Shoals Falls Trail, which has different mileage notations, according to whether you hike the loop route, take side spur trails, or just hike to the falls and back. Even the shortest in and out hike of about 3 miles will take about an hour's hiking time. Hiking counterclockwise, the first section of the trail is an old logging road, relatively easy, following along the creek with rushing cascades and bridge crossings. The last section of the trail grows steep and has a lot of rock and wood stairs, some high and hard to climb, before reaching the overlook for the falls, which drops 80 feet into rocks and pools below. Here, at this scenic spot, you can take a short rest, turn around to return, or continue on the longer loop trail. Along this route watch for side trails leading 0.2-mile to Big Bear Falls and to Upper Falls Cascades. There are many more trails to choose from, most all interior trails, linking off other trails.

You could spend days here hiking all the trails and enjoying many outdoor adventures. There are twenty backcountry campsites in six areas of the park and a drive-to family camp area with eighteen sites and a bathhouse nearer the visitor center. Other RV-friendly campgrounds and rental cabins are scattered around the area, most not far from the park. The park is also readily accessible to Asheville and the Blue Ridge Parkway.

Lake James State Park

Mountains Region - Burke & McDowell Counties
Park Address: 2785 NC-126, Nebo, NC 28761
Park Size: 3,743 acres   Month Visited: May
Directions: From I-40 take Exit 90, heading north on Harmony
Grove Road. Stay right on Harmony Grove at intersection and
continue north. After crossing Hwy 70 at Nebo, turn right and east
on NC Hwy 126. Follow for 2.3 miles to the Catawba Access and
park office.

Park Description:

      Lake James is a large reservoir in the mountains of North Carolina. The
lake was created by the Duke Power Company in the early 1900s, through dam-
ming of the Linville and Catawba rivers and Paddy Creek, and the park is named
for one of the company's founders, James Buchanan Duke. The beautiful 6,510-
acre lake has 150 miles of shoreline and is the centerpiece of the park which
opened in 1987. Lake James State Park is often called a "Two-in-One" park because it has two major developed park areas, each with visitor centers, and a
wealth of amenities like boating, fishing, swimming, picnicking, camping, hiking
and biking trails, paddling, and more.

      Coming up Hwy 126 from Nebo brings you first to the Catawba River
Area of the park, named for the American Indians who once lived here. This is

the older developed section on the southern end of the lake. Because the park is large and spread out, a stop at the park office and visitor center is wise to get information, a park map, and needed directions. Behind the visitor center is a beautiful broad sandy swim beach with a bathhouse, canoe and kayak boat rentals, picnic tables and pavilions, all ready for a nice day on the water. A short 0.3-

mile trail leads to a big fishing pier. Anglers love fishing off the pier, banks, or from boats on the lake. The cool, deep waters provide good fishing with large-mouth bass, white bass, crappie, bluegill, catfish, and others in abundance. Two fine boat launches are only a short distance down Hwy 126 at the Canal Bridge Boat Ramp and at the Paddy's Creek Park area.

The park has a rich abundance of hiking trails in all sections. The Fishing Pier Trail leads past the fishing pier to link into the 2.2-mile Fox Den Trail, winding through a scenic woodland. Across from the visitor center another trail, the half mile Sandy Cliff Overlook Trail, follows out a long finger in the lake to a wooden overlook with gorgeous views across the lake. Near the beginning of this trail, by a wooden bridge, a side trail curls over to the park campground, as does a nearby side road. The family campground is a small walk-in camp loop with a bathhouse

and sites for tents or trailers, but with no electric and water hookups. However, several nearby resorts have large, fully-equipped RV sites. Another pretty trail starting by the campground, the 1.5-mile Lake Channel Overlook Trail, twines out another finger of the lake to an outdoor amphitheater and to a second pretty overlook point.

From the Catawba River Area, Hwy-126 leads past the two boat docks and then over a bridge to the newer and larger Paddy's Creek Area. Follow the road into the park to its end to the large visitor center which sits on a hillside looking out over the lake. Here, you'll find another swim beach, much like the one at Catawba, a bathhouse, picnic tables, pavilions, and a fishing pier, all in a lovely setting. A waterside trail winds out from this main area, the 1.0-mile Paddy's Creek Trail that leads along a channel of Lake James. This trail links into several other park trails, the 0.7-mile Homestead Trail and the Mill's Creek Trail that circles back through the Campground Area.

The campground here is a larger one than at Catawba with 33 sites you can drive into for tent and trailer camping, with a bathhouse centrally located to all. These sites, like at Catawba, are non-electric but all are well- equipped with grills and tables. Across the water from the Paddy's Creek Campground are 30 campsites scattered on the Long Arm Peninsula, accessible only by boat and perfect for paddle-in camping. Each has a fire pit, picnic table, and a 16-foot tent pad. These sites are more remote but beautiful and not far from the shoreline.

The Paddy's Creek Area is unique in that it has a big network of Mountain Bike trails. The Lower and Upper Tindo trails, 1.4-miles each, are best for beginners, while intermediate and more experienced bikers will love the longer 4.4-miles East Wimbo and the 6.0 miles West Wimba loops. These well-main-

150

tained trails weave back into the less developed part of the park and can be interlinked for miles of good biking fun.

Near the Paddy's Creek entrance is a pullover parking space at the 0.75-mile Holly Discovery Trail, starting under a wooden arch. This is a fun trail for children with informational signage along its route to teach more about plants and animals. Across the creek from this trail is the 2.0-mile Overmountain Victory Trail that follows a short piece of the 225-miles long route the Overmountain Men followed in 1780 to fight the British at Kings Mountain in the Revolutionary War. It's easy to find an abundance of things to do and see in this interesting park. And nearby are the Blue Ridge Mountains and many other scenic attractions.

Overmountain Victory National Historic Trail

Park Address: NC Div. of Parks & Recreation, 1615 Mail Service Center, Raleigh, NC 27699
Park Size: 225 trail miles in NC   Month Visited: March
Directions: The NC section of the Overmountain Historic Trail begins on the eastern TN/NC border in Avery County, and at Elkin in Surry County, NC, to merge at Morganton, NC in Burke County and travel to the NC/SC border in Rutherfordton County.

Park Description:

Photo: Pam Mulinix

The Overmountain Victory National Historic Trail is governed by the National Park system and stretches roughly 330 miles from points in Tennessee and Virginia through North Carolina to South Carolina. The trail follows the paths the American Patriot Militia took, during the Revolutionary War, as they mustered to fight the British at the Battle of Kings Mountain in 1780. The North Carolina Division of Parks and Recreation works with the National Parks system to manage and maintain the 225-mile trails section crossing through North Carolina. The Overmountain Men, largely a group of 1,100 volunteers versus being trained soldiers, traveled this long route on foot for love of freedom and love of country. Every year the Overmountain Victory Trail Association re-enacts the march in entirety. Additionally, local groups do re-enactments at different points along the trail during the year to remember specific dates.

There are sites all along the trail route that visitors can see and enjoy, and there are several accessible pieces of the trail interested individuals can hike on. The Overmountain Men from Virginia and Tennessee marched to cross the Watauga River at Sycamore Shoals and to muster there at Elizabethton, TN, at the fort before moving on. It isn't far over the border of North Carolina to visit this fort and see historic sites related to the march's beginning. We explored the fort and museum and then also visited Roan Mountain where the Overmountain Men marched over into

North Carolina. On the Blue Ridge Parkway, we stopped at Gillespie Gap in Spruce Pine, NC, where the Overmountain Men also crossed, locating the Overmountain Trail markers adjacent to the Museum of North Carolina Minerals and viewing the informative Overmountain display inside the Museum.

While visiting Lake James State Park, we walked a two-mile piece of the Overmountain Trail within the park. Near the park, the second band of Overmountain Men, coming from Elkin and Wilkesboro, NC, converged with the Overmountain Men from Tennessee at the McDowell House in present-day Morganton, built by Captain Charles McDowell, Jr, who was a leader of the patriots. His home in Morganton can be visited and is now on the National Register of Historic Places. The men headed south next from this point, through Rutherfordton and into South Carolina near Chesnee before turning east to head to Kings Mountain.

In South Carolina, we stopped at Cowpens where another critical American victory took place, later in 1781, and then moved on to Kings Mountain. We visited the museum at the Kings Mountain Military Park, watched the film there, and learned about the battle of Kings Moun-

tain fought October 7th, 1780, the first major patriot victory to occur after the invasion of Charleston by the British. The battle has often been called "the war's largest all-American fight."

Photo: Pam Mulinix

As you travel through North Carolina, and even in Tennessee and South Carolina, you may want to stop and see some of these Overmountain sites along the way and walk the pathways some of these brave patriots once walked.

153

Blue Ridge Parkway National Parkway

Mountains Region
Park Address: Park Headquarters, 199 Hemphill Knob Rd, Asheville, NC 28803
Park Size: appx 252-mi in NC   Month Visited: Oct & March
Directions: To reach the Park Headquartes Visitor Center at Asheville, from I-40, take Exit 53B onto Alt Hwy 74 south to left onto Blue Ridge Parkway. Follow to left on Hemphill Knob Road to the Parkway Corporate Office and main Visitor Center.

Park Description:

     The Blue Ridge Parkway travels for 469 miles from its start at Rockfish Gap, VA, in the Shenandoah Mountains to its end at Cherokee, NC, in the Great Smoky Mountains. It was the first national rural parkway to be conceived, designed, and constructed in the U.S. for a leisure-type driving experience. Work to build the parkway started in 1935, with approximately half the parkway finished before World War II, and with the last missing link section, skirting Grandfather Mountain at Linn Cove, completed in 1987. The mammoth project took over 52 years to complete and is a beautiful roadway to drive. Stanley Abbott, the Chief Landscape Architect for the Parkway said, "The idea is to fit the Parkway into the mountains as if nature has put it there"—and that is how visitors feel as they drive this beautiful stretch of road.

It takes more than a day to drive and enjoy the parkway, either in its entirety or only driving the North Carolina sections, with the speed limit 45 miles per hour at the max and occasionally dropping to 25-35 mph. Additionally, visitors will want to savor the drive, making stops to scenic overlooks and interesting sites along the way. We traveled most of the parkway over the last two years as

we worked on visiting North Carolina's state parks, so you will see an assortment of seasonal photo memories in illustration of the route from north to south.

The Blue Ridge Parkway passes into North Carolina below Roanoke, VA, at Milepost 216.9 at the state line, soon coming to Cumberland Knob, Milepost 217.5, a spot called "the birthplace of the Blue Ridge Parkway." A sign tells you this site was the first recreational development on the parkway and built by the Civilian Conservation Corps in the 1930s. Like at many of the main milepost points, there is a visitor center here, a picnic area and a couple of trails to hike. Not far after Cumberland Gap, the parkway drives by Stone Mountain State Park, that we explored and visited, then passes Bluff Mountain and the

Northwest Trading Post at Milepost 258.6 not far from Mount Jefferson State Park, another of our stops. The Parkway next crosses Deep Gap at Milepost 276.4 with turnoffs to Boone and Blowing Rock.

Near Boone we visited Elk Knob State Park and at Blowing Rock we stopped at the Moses H. Cone Memorial Park and Visitor Center at Milepost 292 and at nearby Julian Price Memorial Park where you can see pretty Price Lake from the Parkway. Driving on, we passed over the Linn Cove Viaduct at Milepost 304.4. Soon after is the Linville Falls Visitor Center at Milepost 316.4 with turns off the Parkway after that lead to three-tiered 2,000-foot Linville Falls and the 12,000-acre Linville Gorge, known as the Grand Canyon of the Southern Appalachians. This is a side trip not to miss and there is also a campground, trails, and a picnic area here on the Linville River. It's about 3 miles south from the Parkway to Linville Falls and 24 miles to Marion, NC, which is close to Lake James State Park we explored and visited.

Not far south on the Parkway is the turn at Milepost 331 to the Museum of North Carolina Minerals, which contains another Visitor Center, an interesting museum and memorial point where the Overmountain Men crossed in the Revolutionary War. For a nice short hike, stop next at Crabtree Falls Overlook at Milepost 339.5, where a trail leads from the campground to a sixty-foot falls. Next on our parkway agenda was a visit to Mount Mitchell State Park at Milepost 355.4 and beyond it a stop at Craggy Gardens at Milepost 364.4 where there is a nice picnic area. In summer a 1.5-mile round trip walk up Craggy Pinnacle Trail leads to incredible vistas and a glory of purple rhododendrons in late June.

Beyond Asheville is the park's main headquarters and visitor center and then Mount Pisgah at Milepost 408.6 with trails, a picnic area, campground, inn and restaurant—all once a part of the Vanderbilt estate. Several lovely overlooks follow off Graveyard Fields and Looking Glass Rock as the Parkway winds through the Nantahala National Forest and to Waterrock Knob at Milepost 451.2, where there is another visitor center. The road then moves into the Great Smoky Mountains. Scenic points abound along this stunning mountain section of the parkway, which passes the side road to Balsam Mountain campground and trails at Heintooga Ridge, to drop gradually into Cherokee at the Southern end of the Blue Ridge—a lovely satisfying trip.

Mount Mitchell State Park

Mountains Region - Yancey County
Park Address: 2388 State Hwy 128, Burnsville, NC 28644
Park Size: 1,855 acres   Month Visited: March
Directions: From Asheville, NC, or from any access point, get on the Blue Ridge Parkway and follow to Milepost # 355 amd turn north on NC Hwy 128 which leads directly into the park.

Park Description:

Mount Mitchell is an extraordinary place. The Cherokee Indians once used the area as a hunting ground before white settlers came, and then timber companies created roads and a railroad up the mountain for logging. In the early 1900s, a lumber company brought passengers up the mountain for extra money. After hiking to the summit and seeing the stunning beauty of the area, the people of North Carolina began to write their newspapers and politicians to save the land around the summit. In 1915 their voices were heard and Mount Mitchell became North Carolina's first state park. It is named for Elisha Mitchell who explored the mountain summit and determined it the highest peak in the eastern United States, at 6,684 feet.

As you drive up Hwy 128 into the park, you'll cross the Mountains-to-Sea-Trail and then pass Mt. Gibbes and Mt. Hallback to the left before arriving at the Park Office and Visitor Center, where you can snag a map, needed information, and park brochures. Behind the center several of the park's trails begin. The easier walk to explore is the two-mile Commissary Trail leading to Camp Alice, once an old logging camp and railroad stop. Tourists would arrive here on the train and then walk from Camp Alice to the summit.

The Mount Mitchell State Park Restaurant sits a half mile from the park office at Stepps Gap, open from May through October, and offering a varied menu for breakfast, lunch, or dinner and stupendous views. I loved the rocking chairs on the porch here where you could sit and look out over the mountain. From the restaurant parking lot, the two-mile Old Mitchell hike begins, offering a strenuous climb to the summit. The narrow trail gains 6,000 feet in elevation as its climbs with rock steps and difficult sections along the way but also with scenic vistas and rugged beauty.

Continuing up the highway leads to a walk-in tent camping area on the left with nine sites. These sit along a scenic pathway leading to a spur trail, the sites non-electric, but with water spigots and a nice restroom. There are other primitive camping areas scattered around the park off the backcountry trails.

At the road's end is a large parking area and a raised rock observation patio offering stunning views out over the mountain below and beyond that will take your breath away. After enjoying the views, walk down to see the Mount Mitchell Museum with its interesting historical and geological exhibits. Visitors will find a life-size figure of mountain explorer big Tom Wilson and a replica of his cabin. Other exhibits include an interactive weather station, geology section about rock types in the park, dioramas of animals and plant life, and a topographical map.

Adjacent to the parking lot is a gift shop, restrooms, and concessions stand. A short distance above on the hillside is a shady picnic area with forty tables and two rustic and picturesque picnic pavilions. Several trails begin from this area. A short Balsam Nature Loop winds for less than a mile from the parking lot to some great views, and for a longer strenuous hike, the almost twelve-mile Black Mountain Crest Trail heads deeper into the mountain to connect to several other trails for a more wilderness adventure. To admire the incredible views or hike on a mountain trail, Mount Mitchell is a park you will long remember.

Grandfather Mountain State Park

Mountains Region- Avery, Caldwell and Watauga Counties
Park Address: 9872 Highway 105 South, Banner Elk, NC 28644
Park Size: 2,456 acres   Month Visited: March
Directions: From Highway 321 in Boone, NC, take Hwy 105
and drive approximately 10 minutes to the interim park office in
Grandfather View Village on right.

Park Description:

The first quick differentiation to make in introducing this new state park, opened in 2009, is that it is not the same as the well-known Grandfather Mountain attraction with its Mile-High Swinging Bridge. Although this nearby attraction, off the Blue Ridge Parkway on Hwy 221, adjoins the Grandfather Mountain State Park, the two facilities are separate entities. The Grandfather Mountain attraction offers, for a ticket price, a wide variety of amenities and entertainments like the mile-high bridge, a wildlife habitat, nature center, café, picnic areas, and access points into the park. The Morton family, who owned all of Grandfather Mountain for six decades, transferred the bulk of their property to North Carolina for a park in 2008.

The Grandfather Mountain State Park, being one of the state's newest properties, is still in developmental stages. Mostly undeveloped wilderness at this time, the park is a hiker's paradise with thirteen miles of trails in challenging terrain, backcountry camping sites, and incredible views from high points on the mountain. The park has two access areas to its trails at this time. The temporary park office can be found on the western side of the mountain on Highway 105 in the Grandfather View Village, 3.5-miles from the Profile Trail parking lot. The other access point can be found on the east side of the mountain off the Blue Ridge Parkway.

The Profile Trail is a 3.6-mile (7.2 RT) strenuous trail, rising steadily uphill to connect at Calloway Gap with the Grandfather Trail on the crest of Grandfather Mountain. The climb, from 4,034 feet to

5,675 feet at the gap, takes four hours to complete even for seasoned hikers. The trail begins on a scenic pathway, crosses the Watauga River and rises higher and higher to pass the famous "Grandfather Profile" on a rock face, that the mountain is named for. It then moves through boulders and clamors up rock steps to the gap with many incredible views along the route. Continuing north along the mountain's

crest leads to Calloway Peak, at 5,946 feet, one of the highest peaks in the Blue Ridge range. Several backcountry campsites can be found in this area and the Balsam Shelter.

The second access point into the park's trails is on the Blue Ridge Parkway at Milepost 299.9 at the Boone Fork Overlook parking lot. A moderate trail to explore is the 1.2-mile (2.4 mi RT) Nuwati Trail. First follow the ongoing Tamawha Trail from the parking lot to the trailhead. After approximately 0.25 mile, the Niwati Trail turns right on an old logging road. The ongoing rocky trail crosses a stream before rising to a high view point, where hikers can view Storytellers Rock, the ridges of Grandfather Mountain, and scenes into the valley below. To expand your hike, the 0.4-mile Cragway Trail connects over to the Daniel Boone Scout Trail, but even though short it is narrow, steep, and strenuous. For a still longer day, the Boone trail, continues along the mountain to Calloway Peak, passing the Balsam Shelter and camping sites along its route.

Continuing south on the Parkway, several Overlooks offer stupendous views of Grandfather's Mountain, MacRae Peak and other high points. A nice place to stop after exploring the park trails is at the Linn Cove Visitor Center, where there are exhibits, a gift shop, picnic tables, and restrooms in a beautiful facility with fine overlooks.

Not far beyond the visitor center at Milepost 305, is the turn on Highway 221 to the

Grandfather Mountain scenic travel attraction, operated by the Grandfather Mountain Stewardship Foundation. Here guests pay an admission fee to drive through the park attraction and enjoy its amenities. Be advised it is best to buy tickets to the attraction in advance via online reservation at the Grandfather Mountain Attraction website at: *grandfather.com/tickets*. Daily tickets are limited and sell out quickly, especially on weekends and during peak tourist seasons. After stopping at the main gate to confirm your tickets, begin the two-mile drive up to Grandfather Mountain summit.

On the right, at appx 0.5-mile, a right turn leads into a nice picnic area where you will also find the Woods Walk Trail, a short, easy walk for all ages. The road then winds on upward to a left turn at the nature museum, the Wilson Center of Nature Discovery and the Animal Habitat behind it. The museum is filled with over a dozen interesting exhibits as well as a small café where you can have lunch or a snack. While at the museum you can see a free film in the Hodges Theater and enjoy scheduled nature education programs. Outdoors is a pavilion and botanical garden, plus the Animal Wildlife Habitats. Here, in large, natural enclosures, you can see bears, cougars, eagles, otters, and elk.

Continuing on up the road leads to a hiking parking area which offers access to several of Grandfather Mountain's hiking trails. One, the 0.4-mile Bridge Trail, winds all the way up to the Swinging Bridge, meeting other trails along its route, while the other, the 1.0-mile Black Rock Trail winds out from the back of the parking lot to Arch Rock and Grandfather View. After more twists and turns, the ongoing road arrives at the parking lot at the top of the mountain. Here, in a large building called Top Shop, is a visitor center and gift shop, exhibit room, and

an elevator which leads to the 50-foot walkway and the Mile-High Swinging Bridge. Beyond the visitor center, a rocky stairway also leads up to the bridge. The 228-foot mile high suspension bridge, at 5,303 feet, crosses an 80-foot chasm, offering 360-degree panoramic views of Grandfather Mountain at 5,946 feet and vistas of other high summits. Bring your camera for great photo memories from this stunning high mountain top.

Across from the Top Shop several more hiking trails begin. Be aware that the trails here are rocky and challenging and require careful footwork. Many have boulders, cables, and ladders to climb to reach rocky overlooks. The 2.4-mile Grandfather Trail along the mountain's crest to MacRae Peak, Attic Window, and Calloway Peak is difficult

and advised for only experienced hikers. All these high trails are more challenging than most hikers are used to and can be dangerous. So use caution if you explore them. A map of the trails can be attained at the Grandfather Mountain Attraction or at the State Park Office.

Carl Sandburg National Historic Site

Mountains Region - Henderson County
Park Address: 1800 Little River Road, Flat Rock, NC 28731
Park Size: 270 acres   Month Visited: May
Directions: From I-26, turn south on US Hwy 64 to Hendersonville and then left and south on Hwy 225. At Flat Rock, turn right and west on Little River Road and follow to park.

Park Description:

This National Historic Site memorializes the home of Carl August Sandburg (1878-1967), an American poet, journalist, historian, editor, and performer. Often compared to Walt Whitman in his use of free verse, Sandburg won two Pulitzer Prizes for his books of poetry and another for his history of President Abraham Lincoln's life. Sandburg's parents were Swedish immigrants and his early years were filled with interrupted schooling and an assortment of jobs to help support his family. After serving in the Spanish American War, he attended college and then began to work for newspapers.

He married Lillian "Paula" Steichen and they had three daughters. In 1945, the family moved to Flat Rock, North Carolina, to a farm estate they named Connemara. Sandburg lived here until his death and wrote one-third of his works while at Connemara. At his wife's Lillian's death, she left Connemara and the estate to North Carolina for a historic site. Sandburg was a prolific writer and in addition to his many books of poetry he wrote historical pieces, children's books, folklore, and songs.

It is an interesting learning experience to visit Connemara and to learn more about Carl and Lillian Sandburg, their daughters Margaret, Janet, and Helga and to walk the beautiful grounds around their home. After parking, visitors walk in on a winding road into the farm, passing by Front Lake. The main home of the Sandburg's soon comes into view and inside is the visitor center and park store. Tours are given on specified days and times,

which can be found with other information on the National Park website.

After visiting the house, take a walk to the Connemara Farms Goat Dairy, Mrs. Sandburg's love and passion. Here you can see the pretty red barns and buildings and see descendants of Lillian Sandburg's goats. While daughter Margaret became a great help to her father editing his writing, Janet and Helga loved the farm and the animals, and loved working with the goat dairy. Mrs. Sandburg was a prize-winning and acclaimed pioneer of the American dairy goat industry and bred many champion goats.

Rich in history, this a picturesque park you won't want to miss and easy to get to near Hendersonville and Asheville, North Carolina. The Connemara estate includes a trout pond, duck pond, manager's home and tenant house, and many outbuildings. It is a pleasure to explore the property and to learn how the Sandburg family lived.

Many trails wind around the estate from easy ones to more strenuous ones. Most have rest benches along the way so visitors can sit and enjoy the natural settings. Two trails, the 3.5 miles Memminger Trail Loop and the 3.4-miles Big Glass Trail both lead to overlooks of Glassy Mountain at 2,783 feet. The Memminger Trail also has a view of Little Glassy Mountain, along its route. For an easy walk the approximately half mile Front Lake Trail loops along the lake in front of the house and the simple Trout Pond Trail is even shorter. A moderate trail to walk, is the approximately 1-mile Little Glassy Mountain Trail, starting and ending at the family home.

Chimney Rock State Park

Mountains Region - Rutherford County
Park Address: 743 Chimney Park Rd, Chimney Rock, NC 28720
Park Size: 8,014 acres   Month Visited: May
Directions: From Interstate 40 near Asheville, take Alternate Hwy 74 and follow to Main Street in town of Chimney Rock. Turn right at Chimney Park Road to the main park office.

Park Description:

     This beautiful and popular park is home to majestic mountain scenery and the 315-foot granite monolith, called Chimney Rock, that the park is named for. This outcropping, that looks like a tall rock chimney rising into the sky, sits at 2,280 feet above sea level and the views from its well-known overlook draw visitors from all over the world.

     The park was established in 2005 as Hickory Nut Gorge State Park but when the state bought the tourist addition of Chimney Rock Park from the Morse family in 2007, the park was renamed Chimney Rock State Park. An admission fee is charged for entrance into the attraction portion of the park and fee rates and hours can be found on the state park website. The park can get very busy during tourist seasons and it is wise to plan your trip accordingly.

     There is no fee to hike or explore in the other areas of the park, home to mostly rugged hiking trails and backcountry. The state park has two access areas,

at this time, besides the Chimney Rock attraction—Rumbling Bald Access and Eagle Rock Access. The rest of the park is as yet undeveloped but there are plans for more trails and amenities. The State Park Office is on Chimney Rock Park Road before the ticket entrance, where information about the trails can be attained.

Rumbling Bald Access is not far from the main park, off Boys Camp Road, about two miles east of the park entrance. From the parking area, Rumbling Bald Trail winds in a 3-mile roundtrip loop through boulder fields with some fine scenic views. Eagle Rock Access, the second access area, can be found at the end of Shumont Road off Hwy 9. Part of the 17-mile Weed Patch Mountain Trail runs within the park boundary and this trail is for both hikers and bikers. Also, the 1.5-mile short and strenuous Tunnel Trail branches off of this trail to make its way through rough terrain and a rocky tunnel.

For most visitors, the main Chimney Rock Access is the most popular draw. This is the area we visited on our trip. I first enjoyed simply driving in to the charming little tourist town of Chimney Rock, set along a mountain stream and reminding me of Gatlinburg near my home. The entrance to the park is found right in the middle of town, the park road turning between historic rock buildings and then crossing the Rocky Broad River. We paused and took time to enjoy the tumbling mountain stream and to walk along the short Riverwalk Trail near the park entrance. Next, we stopped at the main park entry building on the left to pick up a map and brochures before passing through the ticket plaza and heading into the park.

Wanting to see everything on our way up the three-mile road to the upper parking lot, we stopped next at the lower parking lot to see the picnic and pavil-

ion area, outdoors classroom, and the Animal Discovery Den. Then we had fun walking around the Great Woodland Trail. This charming half-mile loop trail has statuary and interpretive stations along the way, some hands-on stations, and it was interesting to learn about the animals that inhabit the park. This is a great trail for kids and the young-at-heart.

Across the road we checked out the Four Seasons Trail, about a mile in length (2-mi RT). Like most of the park trails it has a lot of climbs, this one rising over 400 feet, with a lot of stairs, but also with some lovely viewpoints along the route before ending into another trail. Returning to our car, we headed back up the park road to the upper parking lot enjoying the scenery along the way.

At the road's end is a gift shop, concessions area, and restrooms and an option to walk or take the elevator to the top of Chimney Rock. A sign says "Choose Your Path of Adventure to the Chimney" but be warned there are about 500 stairs on the trail to the Outcroppings Overlook at Chimney Rock, not the wisest choice for novice hikers or anyone with health conditions. Do take a short walk up the steps to the overlook and to see Gneiss Cave.

We opted to take the elevator up higher, which dropped us at the top where we could walk along a lovely wooden walkway enjoying the fantastic views. A pretty side overlook offers views out over Hickory Gorge, Lake Lure and the surrounding mountain ranges. At the end of the walkway, you

can walk up 47 stairs to the top of Chimney Rock for even more breathtaking panoramas at a second overlook high in the sky. Another short but strenuous trail, with many more steps to climb, leads to more viewpoints like the Opera Box and

168

Devil's Head before reaching Exclamation Point. Beyond it, the Skyline Trail leads across the bluff for about a mile.

We finished our park visit by walking the 1.7-mile trail to Hickory Nut Falls. It takes about 45 minutes to complete and leads to one of the highest waterfalls east of the Mississippi. The long cascade drops 404-feet over the side of a rocky cliff. There is a wooden overlook near the base of the falls with nice rest benches – a good ending spot to our day at this beautiful park. It is easy to see why this park is so beloved by all who visit.

Appalachian National Scenic Trail

Park Address: App. Trail Conservancy, 160A Zillicoa St., Asheville, NC 28801

Park Size: 320.4 mi in NC   Month Visited: August

Directions: In North Carolina, the Appalachian Trail runs from below the VA/NC border at Roan Mtn all the way to the NC/GA border near Bly Gap.

Park Description:

The Appalachian Trail (AT) is the longest "hiking-only" footpath in the world. The entire trail stretches more than 2,000 miles from its beginning at Springer Mountain in Georgia to Mount Katahdin in Maine. From GA the trail enters the state of NC at Bly Gap near the border and travels for over 320 miles through the state, 95.7 miles in NC and 224.7 miles on the border between NC and Tennessee. The idea for the trail was conceived in 1921, built by private citizens, and completed in 1937. The AT is managed by the National Park Service, Appalachian Trail Conservancy, and the U.S. Forest Service. A detailed map of the Appalachian Trail sections in NC can be found on the NC National Park Website.

The Appalachian Trail does not have a Visitor Center but books and websites give good information about the trails. Many access points to the Appalachian Trail are not difficult to find for an exploration walk on a part of this famous national trail. At the northern end of the AT several trails branch out from Carvers Gap at Roan Mountain. The trail to Grassy Ridge Bald is a nice 4.7-mile hike, rolling its way over three balds to reach Grassy Ridge at 6,100-ft, with lovely panoramic views. This is the longest stretch of grassy bald in the Appalachian Mountains. A little further south, and east of Asheville, another popular trail, the 1.5-mile Max Patch hike leads to yet another glorious bald with 360-degree panoramas.

At Davenport Gap, the Appalachian Trail (AT) crosses Interstate 40 and begins to follow the TN/NC border across the Great

Smoky Mountains. This section of the trail is near our home and we have hiked many of the pieces of the AT in the Smokies. In the Deep Creek area, a number of trails lead to the AT. Chestnut Branch Trail connects to the AT in 2.1-miles to climb on upward to the Mt Cammerer tower. The Low Gap Trail off the Big Creek Trail, one of our favorites, also connects to the AT after

2.5-miles up a delightful streamside trail. From the TN Cosby Campground, several trails travel to connect to the AT, also, including the other end of Low Gap Trail, the 4.6-mile Snake Den Ridge Trail, and the 7.4-mile Mount Cammerer Trail.

At the very top of the Smoky Mountains, above Gatlinburg, at Newfound Gap where the AT crosses, hikers can take the popular 8-mi RT hike to a precipice called Charlie's Bunion with spectacular viewpoints, More access points directly into the AT can be found at the Clingman's Dome parking lot nearby, like the trail out to Mt. Buckley and Silers Bald. From other points on the TN side of the Smokies, popular trails rise to meet the AT, too, like the Bote Mountain and Russell Field trails near Cades Cove.

As the AT eventually leaves the high Smokies ridges, it walks directly across Fontana Dam, the tallest dam in the eastern U.S., before continuing on its way. The AT then winds south into the Nantahala Forest and into an extensive wilderness area. At the well-known Nantahala Center, the trail crosses over the river bridge before winding south again.

Two final hikes, not difficult to get to before the AT leaves the state, can be found at the Wayah Gap picnic area, where a 3.6 mi trail leads to Siler Bald with glorious views and at Deep Gap near the border where a strenuous trail climbs to Standing Indian Mountain.

Enjoy sampling the many AT trails in North Carolina.

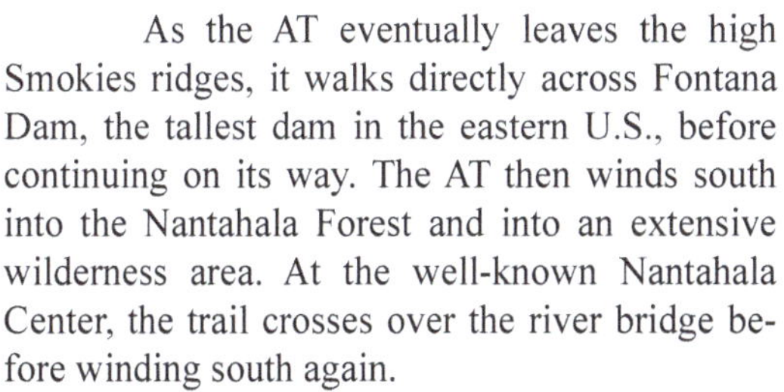

Rendezvous Mountain State Park

Mountains Region - Wilkes County
Park Address: 1956 Rendezvous Mtn Rd, Purlear, NC 28665
Park Size: 1,800 acres   Month Visited: March
Directions: Travel U.S. Hwy 421 to Wilkesboro and take NC Hwy 16 north. Turn left onto Shingle Gap Road and then onto Rendezvous Mountain Road into the park.

Park Description:

In actuality, Rendezvous was originally one of North Carolina's earliest state parks, established in 1926. During the Great Depression in the 1930s, the Civilian Conservation Corps (CCC) came and built a road into the park, a cabin and other structures, and worked on trails. Then in 1956 the park was transferred to the Division of Forestry, which later became the North Carolina Forest Service, and the property stayed under their governance until transferred back into the state park system in early 2022. At first the new park operated as a satellite under South Mountain State Park, but in the summer of 2022 it gained a park superintendent of its own.

The park's name came from stories that the Overmountain Men, approximately 200 under Colonel Benjamin Cleveland, used the mountain's summit as a rendezvous point during the Revolutionary War. It is already well-known that a group of the Overmountain Men traveled from upper North Carolina and the Wilkesboro area to join other Overmountain patriots from Tennessee near Morgantown, before heading to the Battle of Kings Mountain in 1780. Because of this history, Judge T.B. Finley donated the original acres to the state in 1926 for a park. Only recently added to the park system, Reneezvous is not well developed yet and the 2-mile entry road to the park is still rough and unpaved but it has a park office, hiking trails, a picnic area, and a fire tower.

Because the park sits at a high elevation, you'll see fine views even entering the park gate. The main road then travels past a small picnic area and Forestry Center. Much of the park was a logging area in its early years and a Logging History Demonstration Trail winds in an 0.6-mile loop to a Sawmill Exhibit area and back. The appx 4-mile Amadahy Trail begins in this area, also, following a steep logging trail to Purlear Creek and a few cascades and waterfalls.

Continuing on up the main road leads to a large parking area at the rustic park office. From the parking lot are more

fine views out across the mountains and valleys below. After visiting the park office, walk across the road to hike the short Talking Tree Trail, an 0.7-mi. loop with interpretive signs along its route and "talking tree" audios, especially nice for kids. This is a well-maintained moderate trail to walk, crossing Purlear Creek along its way. A side trail from the parking area also leads to restrooms, a nice picnic area and a large picnic shelter, built by the CCC, with a beautiful rock chimney in the center of it. There is also a small amphitheater you can take a short walk to, where ranger-led educational programs are held.

Beyond the park office, two gravel roadbeds travel uphill, forming a connection loop near the top as they approach the old fire tower. The Aermotor steel tower, built in 1936 on Rendezvous Mountain's summit, sits at 2,500 feet elevation and is about 60 feet tall. Because of a communications-dish now on top of the tower, that gives off dangerous radio frequencies, the old tower is no longer accessible for climbing and has barriers around it. However, you will find some fine vistas at the road's end. If you don't walk up the northernmost loop of the road, walk back on it as you return to the parking lot to stop and see the old CCC cabin built in the 1930s. The park has few other amenities to explore at this time, so if you visit on a weekday or off season, you may find you have the park almost to yourself since it is off the beaten path and not well-known yet.

Trail of Tears National Historic Trail

Mountains Region
Park Address: NC Trail of Tears Assoc., P.O. Box 607, Whittier, NC 28789 (Jackson County)
Park Size: National Trail 5,045 mi. across nine states
Month Visited: August
Directions: From points in western NC, the Trail of Tears followed various routes leading west to Oklahoma.

Park Description:

The Indian Removal Act of 1830 impacted all Native American nations east of the Mississippi River, but in North Carolina it was the Cherokee who were most impacted. In 1838, despite all the efforts of the Cherokee people to retain their homelands, U.S. military forced all remaining Cherokee off their land, taking them to internment camps where they were held in miserable conditions. From these camps and forts, most were transferred in time to Fort Butler in Murphy, NC, before starting their long, enforced march west. An estimated 4,000 of 15,000 Cherokee died on the journey, giving it the name The Trail of Tears. Those who made the journey west formed the Western Band of Cherokee and those who avoided internment, fled, hid out, or later returned on foot became the Eastern Band of Cherokee in the Qualla Boundary.

Over time, the injustice of the actions taken became recognized and in 1987 the U.S. Congress designated The Trail of Tears a National Historic Trail in memory of those who suffered and died. Many points along the national trail have been recognized and marked, and accessing sites for future inclusion is still ongoing. For accounts of the history of the trail and places to visit in different states, go to the National Park website and to the North Carolina Trail of Tears Association website for excellent information about the trail's history and sites there.

In Western North Carolina, the best place to begin a visit to Trail of Tears sites and to learn more about the trail's history is in Cherokee. Stop first at the Cherokee Welcome Center at 498 Tsali Blvd to see the informational exhibits there and to get an area map to help you find others. Also visit the Museum of the Cherokee Indian nearby to learn more about the Cherokee, their past and the trail. You might also enjoy seeing, in season, the excellent outdoor play *Unto These Hills*, that also

shares the history of the Cherokee in a compelling, award-winning drama.

Around the Western North Carolina area, within driving range of Cherokee, are other points of interest you can visit, all part of the NC Trail of Tears Auto Tour Route. You will find a small park with informational kiosks at several of the fort sites where Cherokee were first taken after capture, like at Fort Delaney in Andrews and Fort Lindsey at Almond. More Trail of Tears Markers are gradually being erected to identify points where the Trail of Tears crossed in NC and nationally. At many locations, you can walk along a trail section the Indians once followed. At the Nantahala Outdoor Center on Hwy 19, near Wesser, you can find one of these markers on the bridge where the Trail once crossed the Nantahala River. There are also markers along old roads once used, like the Great State Road from Franklin to Fort Butler and the Old Army Road connecting Robbinsville and Andrews.

In downtown Murphy on Peachtree Street is the interesting Cherokee County Historical Museum. The museum has an interpretive center for the Trail of Tears, replicas of Cherokee dwellings, a huge collection of Cherokee artifacts, and panels with photos of Cherokee history and culture. Across the Hiwassee River from the museum is the Fort Butler Memorial on a hillside at 170 Fort Butler Street. The extensive fort and its buildings are long gone, but the park has a trail and exhibits reminding all who visit of the thousands of Cherokee prisoners who once passed through this site.

Gorges State Park

Mountains Region - Transylvania County
Park Address:976 Grassy Ridge Road, Sapphire, NC 28720
Park Size: 8,000 + acres   Month Visited: May
Directions: From Interstate 40 at Clyde, exit onto Hwy 74 south.
Follow Hwy 74 to Sylva. Then take Hwy 23 to Franklin, turning
on Hwy 64 south. At Highlands, continue east on Hwy 64 to Sap-
phire. Then turn right on NC Hwy 281 to the park entrance on left.

Park Description:

Gorges State Park is best known for its waterfalls and rugged wilderness
gorges. One of the state's newer parks, it opened in 2009 and is still in developmental stages. The park offers incredible scenic views of the rugged Jocassee
Gorges and has camping facilities, picnicking, fishing, and a wealth of trails for
hiking, biking, and horseback riding.

The park has two access points, one on the east side of the park at Ross-
man, off Hwy 64 on Frozen Creek Road, and the other on the west side of the park
off Hwy 64. The Frozen Creek Road access is the more remote of the two. It has
a parking area, restrooms, and picnic area and is the access point for many of the
park's backcountry trails. The Auger Hole Trail is one of the better-known ones,
a long 14.1-mile trail for hikers, bikers, and equestrians. It winds along Auger
Creek, fords the Toxaway River—there is no bridge—and continues to the park
border. Another trail, the rugged Canebrake Trail, travels to a backcountry

campsite, on a finger of Lake Jocassee, and connects to the long 76-mile Foothills Trail, crossing from South Carolina. Other trails wind off of these, leading to wilderness waterfalls and backcountry campsites.

The more popular and main access to the park is at the Grassy Ridge Access area where the visitor center and the major park amenities are located. The park visitor center

is a beautiful new building with exhibits, meeting rooms, classroom facilities, and a wooden porch on the back with stunning views out over the gorge. A short trail connects to an outdoor amphitheater, while another walks out to a pretty over- look and then on to the picnic area. The picnic area, which can also be accessed via the park loop road sits in a shaded sce- nic spot with picnic tables, pavilions, and restrooms. Across the street is the begin- ning point of one of the park's well-loved hiking trails, the short but steep half-mile- round-trip to Upper Bearwallow Falls. The pathway leads steeply downhill to a wooden observation deck where you can see the 55-foot falls cascading down a long cliff and hillside.

Following the road past the pic- nic area and falls leads to a pullover with another scenic overlook of the gorge. Next down the road is the park's new 13- acre campground. There are 14 sites with

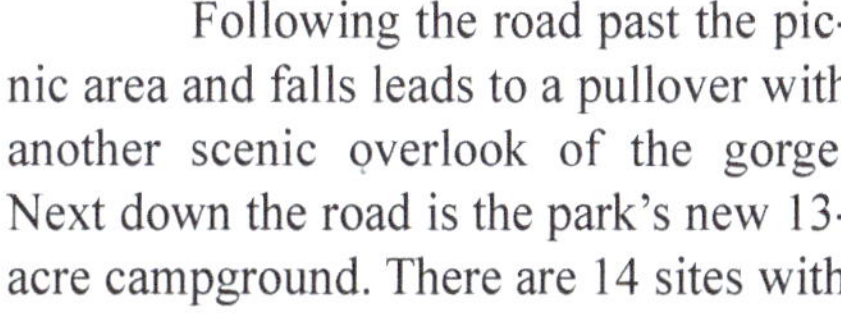

full hookups for RVs and campers, 16 tent sites, showers, restrooms, and a dump station along a wide, paved loop road. The park also has five new rental cabins and all the cabins and camp sites have grills and picnic tables situated on scenic lots.

Not far from the campground is the Grassy Branch Parking area and two more park trailheads. Both start on the same gravel pathway, but at 0.3-mile the Raymond Fisher Trail branches off from the Rainbow Falls Trail. The old logging path follows for 1.5-miles uphill and then down to an overlook across Raymond Fisher Pond. The large pond looks more like a lake in size and beside it is a former campsite area, no longer used—a nice spot for a rest.

The other trail, the Rainbow Falls Trail, is far better known but it is a rougher and much more strenuous hike to take for many. Although it is only 3-miles round trip to the falls overlook and back, the path is difficult, rocky, and not an easy one to walk, with many series of steep stairs before coming to the falls. As the trail reaches Horsepasture River at about a mile and passes into the Pisgah National Forest, the walk grows especially difficult, climbing over boulders, passing through a creek, the ongoing pathway full of roots and rocks. Rainbow Falls at the trail's end, however, is a stunner to see, 150-feet tall and one of the tallest waterfalls in the southeast. Simply standing near this magnificent waterfall and hearing the roar of the water tumbling over the rocks is a thrill.

For the hardy and adventurous, the ongoing trail leads in less than a half mile to another waterfall called Turtleback Falls. This falls tumbles 20-feet over a smooth rock face into a big pool below. In past, people slid down the falls and swam in the pool, but some have also been killed here or swept downstream to their death. So please use care here and at all the falls in the park. A third waterfall, Drift Falls, lies further up the trail, but be aware that this waterfall is now on private property with warning signs to trespassers and should be avoided.

To see an incredible waterfall only 15 minutes from Gorges, follow Hwy 128 south to a well-marked side road to see Whitewater Falls. A short, paved walkway leads to an overlook where you can view this breathtaking cascading waterfall plunging 411 feet, one of the highest waterfalls east of the Rockies. There was a $3 car fee to visit when we went and it was well worth it. Remember, too, that Lake Toxaway and the charming tourist towns of Cashiers, Highlands, and Brevard are not far from Gorges either.

Great Smoky Mountains National Park

Mountains Region - North Carolina
Park Address: 1194 Newfound Gap Road, Cherokee, NC 28719
(Cherokee County)
Park Size: 520,000 acres NC/TN   Month Visited: November
Directions: From Interstate 40 west of Asheville, exit on Hwy 276
to Dellwood. Turn west/right on Hwy 19 and follow to Cherokee.
Then turn north on Hwy 441 and follow to park visitor center at
the entrance to the Smoky Mountains.

Park Description:

On September 2, 1940, President Franklin D. Roosevelt stood at Newfound Gap, with a foot on each side of the Tennessee and North Carolina State line, and dedicated the Great Smoky Mountains National Park. Today because of the love, dedication, and work of hundreds of men and women, who helped to make the park a reality, over 14,000,0000 visitors come to enjoy the park each year. There are over 800 miles of trails for hiking or horseback riding in the park and 70 miles of the Appalachian Trail passes across the mountains. The park also maintains over 80 structures including log buildings, churches, schoolhouses, barns, and working grist mills. It is no surprise the Great Smoky Mountains is the most visited national park in the United States.

The best place to start a visit to

the North Carolina side of the Smokies, often called the "less touristy" side, is to begin at the main Oconoluftee Visitor Center, off Hwy 411 just outside the town of Cherokee. The center has exhibits, a gift shop, and a place to pick up informational brochures and a hiking map. This will help you locate trails of interest and provide a street map to all the different parts of the Smokies. There is a lot to do and see, even just on the North Carolina side of the mountains.

You can start your exploring right beside the visitor center at the Oconoluftee Mountain Village. The farm village has historic buildings to show how families might have lived over 100 years ago. Behind the farm village is the 1.5-mi Oconoluftee River Trail, a lovely walk to take along the river. Nearby, in the Qualla Boundary, is a short trail to stunning 120-foot Mingo Falls, one of the tallest waterfalls in the southeast. Don't forget, also, to explore Cherokee and, especially, to visit the Museum of the Cherokee Indian and the Qualla Arts and Crafts center next door to it.

A short distance from the visitor center, heading north into the Smoky Mountains on Hwy 411, stop at the Mingus Mill, a working turbine grist mill

you can tour. Further up the road is the Smokemont Campground, a nice spot for camping and picnicking. At the end of the campground, several fine hiking trails branch out. One easy to enjoy is the Bradley Fork Trail that follows the stream on a wide roadbed trail. Further up Hwy 411, you'll spot other trails like the Kephart Prong Trail and you can stop at many scenic overlooks, too. The best overlook of all, though, is at the top of the mountain at Newfound Gap. Here, visitors can enjoy stunning views across the North Carolina mountain ranges, hike a piece of the Appalachian Trail that crosses the mountain here, and walk the paved pathway to the 6,643-foot Clingman's Dome observation tower. On a clear day you can see for over 100 miles and across seven states.

Returning down the mountain to Cherokee again, and traveling west on Hwy 19, will take you to Bryson City, NC, and the Deep Creek area of the Smokies. Follow the highway through Bryson City to this beautiful campground tucked under the mountain. From there you can hike many trails into the Smokies, several taking you to waterfalls, like the short Juney Whank Trail, leading to 90-foot Juney Whank Falls. The Deep Creek Trail, a favorite of ours, passes 50-foot Tom Branch Falls and leads to Indian Creek Trail and 60-foot Indian Creek Falls within two miles. Before you leave the area, drive down the "Road to Nowhere" and explore the trails there, and enjoy the charm of Bryson City. You might even want to take a train ride on the Great Smoky Mountain railroad. Traveling further west on Hwy 74 and 23 leads to Fontana Dam and Fontana Village, with views of Fontana Lake along the way. The Appalachian Trail walks directly across the dam coming from high in the Smokies and several trails can be found in this area, like the Lakeview Trail and Twentymile Trail.

Heading east of Cherokee leads to more beautiful Smoky Mountain sites to explore, including Balsam Mountain off the Blue Ridge Parkway, accessed from Cherokee, and trails near Maggie Valley in Cataloochee. The Cataloochee Valley, somewhat like Cades Cove, has historic homes, churches, and old cabins along a scenic road through the valley and also on hiking trails like the Little Cataloochee Trail. We love the Caldwell Fork Trail which starts right next to the Cataloochee Campground. Elk, once extinct, were reintroduced into the valley and visitors now enjoy watching them in the open fields. Above the valley, the Cataloochee Divide Trail winds along the top of the mountain to Purchase Knob and you might wish to stay a night at the Swag, a mountaintop Bed and Breakfast on Hemphill Bald with its incredible viewpoints.

To finish your journey seeing the NC Smokies, follow I-40 northwest from Cataloochee to Waterville and the Big Creek area. You'll find a small campground and picnic area at the end of the road and more hiking trails to explore. Our favorite is the 5.6-miles RT Big Creek Trail, a roadbed trail that follows the stream to the Midnight Hole at 1.4-mile and then to tumbling Mouse Creek Falls at 2.1 miles. The entire Smoky Mountains park is truly a mecca for outdoor lovers, easily accessible, and filled with wonderful things to do and see.

ALPHABETICAL STATE PARK INDEX

Appalchian Trail	170
Blue Ridge Parkway	154
Cape Hatteras National Seashore	32
Cape Lookout National Seashore	36
Carl Sandburg Historic Site	164
Carolina Beach State Park	40
Carvers Creek State Park	82
Chimney Rock State Park	166
Cliffs of the Neuse State Park	76
Crowders Mountain State Park	128
Dismal Swamp State Park	60
Elk Knob State Park	144
Eno River State Park	102
Falls Lake State Park	98
Fort Fisher State Historic Site	44
Fort Macon State Park	48
Fort Raleigh National Historic Site	18
Goose Creek State Park	14
Gorges State Park	176
Grandfather Mountain State Park	160
Great Smoky Mountains Nat'l Park	180
Guilford Courthouse Military Park	110
Hammocks Beach State Park	52
Hanging Rock State Park	120
Haw River State Park	112
Jockey's Ridge State Park	22
Jones Lake State Park	72
Jordan Lake State Park	106
Kerr Lake State Park	90
Lake James State Park	148
Lake Norman State Park	124
Lake Waccamaw State Park	66
Lumber River State Park	64
Mayo River State Park	114
Medoc Mountain State Park	80
Merchants Millpond State Park	62
Moores Creek National Battlefield	54
Morrow Mountain State Park	116
Mount Jefferson State Park	138
Mount Mitchell State Park	158
New River State Park	136
Occoneechee Mountain State Park	104
Overmountain Victory Historic Park	152
Pettigrew State Park	26
Pilot Mountain State Park	132
Raven Rock State Park	84
Rendezvous Mountain State Park	172
Singletary Lake State Park	70
South Mountains State Park	146
Stone Mountain State Park	140
Trail of Tears Historic Trail	174
Weymouth Woods State Park	86
William B. Umstead State Park	94
Wright Brothers National Memorial	30

NORTH CAROLINA STATE PARKS

TIDEWATER REGION

1. Goose Creek State Park
2. Fort Raleigh National Historic Site
3. Jockey's Ridge State Park
4. Pettigrew State Park
5. Wright Brothers National Memorial
6. Cape Hatteras National Seashore
7. Cape Lookout National Seashore
8. Carolina Beach State Park
9. Fort Fisher State Historic Park
10. Fort Macon State Park
11. Hammocks Beach State Park
12. Moores Creek National Battlefield

COASTAL PLAIN REGION

13. Dismal Swamp State Park
14. Merchants Millpond State Park
15. Lumber River State Park
16. Lake Waccamaw State Park
17. Singletary Lake State Park
18. Jones Lake State Park
19. Cliffs of the Neuse State Park
20. Medoc Mountain State Park
21. Carvers Creek State Park
22. Raven Rock State Park
23. Weymouth Woods State Park

PIEDMONT REGION

24. Kerr Lake State Park
25. William B. Umstead State Park
26. Falls Lake State Park
27. Eno River State Park
28. Occoneechee Mountain State Park
29. Jordan Lake State Park
30. Guilford Courthouse National Military Park
31. Haw River State Park
32. Mayo River State Park
33. Morrow Mountain State Park
34. Hanging Rock State Park
35. Lake Norman State Park
36. Crowders Mountain State Park

MOUNTAINS REGION

37. Pilot Mountain State Park
38. New River State Park
39. Mount Jefferson State Park
40. Stone Mountain State Park
41. Elk Knob State Park
42. South Mountains State Park
43. Lake James State Park
44. Overmountain Victory National Historic Trail
45. Blue Ridge Parkway National Park
46. Mount Mitchell State Park
47. Grandfather Mountain State Park
48. Carl Sandburg National Historic Site
49. Chimney Rock State Park
50. Appalachian National Scenic Trail
51. Rendezvous Mountain State Park
52. Trail of Tears National Historic Trail
53. Gorges State Park
54. Great Smoky Mountains National Park

About The Authors

J.L. and Lin Stepp are the co-authors of *Visiting North Carolina State Parks*.

Lin Stepp is a *New York Times* and *USA Today* best-selling international author. A businesswoman and educator, she was on faculty at Tusculum College teaching research and psychology for 20 years, worked in marketing, sales, production art, and regional publishing for over 25 years, and has editorial and writing experience in regional magazines and in the academic field. Stepp writes engaging, heart-warming contemporary Southern fiction with a strong sense of place and has over twenty published novels, each set in different locations around the Smoky Mountains and South Carolina coast. Her past titles include twelve novels in the Smoky Mountain series, five South Carolina coastal novels, and four titles in the new Mountain Home book series, the latest of which are *Eight at the Lake* (2022) and *Seeking Ayita* (2023). In addition she had a novella published in Kensington Publishing's *When the Snow Falls* Christmas anthology and with her husband has co-authored a Smoky Mountains hiking guidebook and three state park guidebooks. For more about her work see: www.linstepp.com

J.L. Stepp is the co-author of the best-selling Smoky Mountain hiking guidebook titled *The Afternoon Hiker* and he and his wife Lin have also co-authored three state park guidebooks *Discovering Tennessee State Parks* (2018), *Exploring South Carolina State Parks* (2021), and *Visiting North Carolina State Parks* (2023). Stepp enjoys a wide variety of outdoor sports, including golf, fishing, and hiking. His background includes over 45 years in sales, marketing, management, and publications. A native East Tennessean and graduate of The University of Tennessee, Stepp owns S & S Communications, established in 1990, which published a monthly outdoor magazine called *Tennessee Fishing & Hunting Guide* for over 30 years. He and his wife Lin travel widely around the southeast region signing at bookstores and festivals and speaking for organizations and events. Contact at: steppcom@aol.com

www.ingramcontent.com/pod-product-compliance
Lightning Source LLC
Chambersburg PA
CBHW040757120726
48005CB00012B/1215